T0106600

IN DEFENSE OF A
NATION

STANLEY GRANT

WestBow
PRESS
A DIVISION OF THOMAS NELSON

WestBow Press books may be ordered through booksellers or by contacting:

WestBow Press
A Division of Thomas Nelson
1663 Liberty Drive
Bloomington, IN 47403
www.westbowpress.com
1-(866) 928-1240

ISBN: 978-1-4497-2917-2 (sc)
ISBN: 978-1-4497-2918-9 (hc)
ISBN: 978-1-4497-2916-5 (e)

Library of Congress Control Number: 2011918740

Printed in the United States of America

WestBow Press rev. date: 10/25/2011

CONTENTS

ACKNOWLEDGMENTS

This book is presented with a grateful heart!
For Murrel and Alli . . . for being terrific editors.
For Ken and Sandra . . . without your help this would only be a dream.
For Toy . . . who taught me two of the most important things I know.
For my father and mother . . .
who taught me how to read the Bible the right way.
For my lovely wife . . . who believes in me.
Thank you one and all! May God bless each of you as you stand in
defense of this great nation!

INTRODUCTION

It is said that America is one nation under God, and rightfully so. John Adams once said, *"Facts are stubborn things; and whatever may be our wishes, our inclinations, or the dictates of our passion, they cannot alter the state of facts and evidence."* When pre-revisionist history speaks for itself, the facts of America's past reveal the God-centered roots of her founding. On November 11, 1620, before the pilgrims disembarked from their ship, they signed a document known as the Mayflower Compact. The intent of their journey to the new world was detailed in its content, which reads in part: *"In the name of God, Amen. We whose names are underwritten . . . having undertaken for the glory of God, and advancement of the Christian faith . . . a voyage to plant the first colony in the northern parts of Virginia."* Thus our nation began, and this position is reflected in the writings of the original framers, regardless of their denomination of worship. From our birth and the Revolutionary War cry of *"No king but King Jesus"*, to Supreme Court rulings declaring America to be a *"Christian nation"* (1892 Church of the Holy Trinity vs. the United States), we find overwhelming evidence of our national purpose . . . to be one nation under God.

Even our form of government is inspired by the Bible. _Isaiah 33:22_ reads _"For the LORD is our judge, the LORD is our lawgiver, the LORD is our king; he will save us."_ The recreational reader quickly misses the fact that three branches of government are represented in this verse: The Judicial branch (the LORD as judge), the Legislative branch (the LORD as lawgiver), and the Executive branch (the LORD as king). Our forefathers, however, were not recreational users, and they viewed this division of power as America's saving grace. With a fresh taste of oppression and a healthy fear of lawlessness, they aimed for a government somewhere between leftist tyranny and rightist anarchy. The result was a Constitutional Republic in the middle of the political spectrum; a Christian nation governed by law yet affording people the freedom to do what is right under God.

On matters of liberty, they believed that unalienable rights are given to humanity by God, and not by government. Consequently, government was handcuffed and given no authority to sanction or disembowel the laws of nature and of nature's God. For a Christian people, government is always the lesser authority, not the final authority, and this kept the American people free from tyranny. On matters of order, they balanced liberty with law, and stressed that our rights must only be exercised within the rule of law . . . God's law. This kept us from drifting into anarchy and lawlessness, which eventually always give rise to a new form of tyranny.

This is the real America! In contrast to revisionist America, real America stands in stark contrast to any system of tyranny detailed in scripture or secular history books. When there's a global crisis, America is there to help. The humanitarian reach of America is unrivaled by the entire world. When disaster strikes and a nation must rebuild, loans are extended and American money flows. In many cases, those same loans are later forgiven and repayment is never demanded simply because we are a generous people. At home, churches dot the land from sea to shining sea, and we are free to worship on Friday, Saturday, Sunday, or any other day as we see fit. And when historians write of Christian mission endeavors to reach lost souls around the globe, America is at the forefront. We fill the world with food, and many nations today could not exist if it were not for the American farmer. Our Constitution guarantees freedom of religion, freedom of speech, freedom to peaceably assemble, freedom to select our leaders, freedom of the press, and the right to keep and bear arms. And if that's not enough, the 10th Amendment guarantees that the powers not delegated to the United States by the Constitution, nor prohibited by it to the States, are reserved to the States respectively, or to the people. Let freedom ring!

America has become the leader of the free world, and the global community moves largely at her pace. Foreign policies spin around American policies, and all micro economies are pegged to the American dollar. The new word describing America is that of hegemony, which essentially means uncontested dominance. It's a new word for new territory in the history of mankind. Everything rises and falls on the state of America, including the Jewish State of Israel in the Middle East. Nobody is exempt from America's reach, and in spite of our many problems, we are still the land of opportunity.

Frankly, this does not describe a nation birthed and conceived in hell. Nor does it appear that we exist as a mere afterthought in the courts of Heaven. America does not exist because a few Christian pilgrims got lucky and hit the Christian Nation jackpot. No, America exists by design. Divine design. We ARE one nation under God, and if you remove America from the picture, the world has major problems. But that's precisely what the system of antichrist wants. A one-world "problem" allows that system of tyranny to impose its one-world "solution", and we all know, it will not let a perfectly good crisis go to waste. Its political operatives have even informed us to that end.

If you do not believe in the REAL America, you have no position from which to defend her. A right position on national issues comes from understanding God's plan for our nation. Sadly, most Christians today don't think beyond themselves or their church programs. Most people know more about the migration pattern of penguins than they do of the people groups who founded and built our great nation. Because of that, they don't have the foggiest idea who America is in the Bible. If they ever ponder who we may be in the scripture, the prevailing positions of the day tend to revolve around two schools of thought, and both produce a state of blindness. The first school of thought centers on the absence of our nation's name in scripture. From Genesis to Revelation, the single word "America" is nowhere to be found. To that I would agree, but neither are the single words of Russia, China, or Iran; yet they are specifically mentioned in the Bible. They are not mentioned by their modern names because they did not exist under these names at the time the prophets wrote of them. They existed as people groups with different names. But over time they developed as people groups with new names, and they came from the three sons of Noah who segregated and began to propagate after the flood. In truth, all people groups have existed from that time until now, and we just have to know how to find them as we work forward from Genesis, not forward from the present day. If we use Genesis as our starting point, wouldn't it make sense that we the people are in there somewhere?

The second school of thought centers on America's present behavior. That position assumes that due to our present debauchery and sinfulness America was a lucky anomaly in history, but now we are destined to ultimate destruction. We were a blip on the screen, a lucky roll of the dice, an afterthought at best. This position, however, misses a key consideration: When trying to determine the core identity of a people, behavior is not the determining ingredient. Nations are not identified by behavior, but rather by bloodline. Think of it this way: I will always be a Grant, regardless of my behavior. I can choose obedience today, and still be Stan Grant. Or, I can choose to fall off the wagon and commit horrendous sins. As a result I may wake up in a prison cell, but I will still be Stan Grant. How I act will never change who I am. In like manner, Israel of old demonstrated all types of behavior and administrations, both good and bad. In one era, there's the Godly king Hezekiah. In another era, we find the wicked duo of King Ahab and Queen Jezebel. One reign brings blessing, and the other brings judgment. But the nation remained as one nation under God even when they were in the clutches of sin and following a globalist agenda. My point is that national behavior, policy or administration did not change their national identity or God's ownership of them. They were not Israel one day, and Babylon the next. Israel remained Israel regardless of their national sins, and if we expect to uncover the truth of who America is in the Bible, we must turn a blind eye to our present behavior and instead focus on our DNA. As previously stated, our cumulative history does not describe a nation birthed and conceived in hell, nor does it appear that we exist as a mere afterthought in the courts of Heaven. America does not exist because a few Christian pilgrims got lucky and hit the Christian Nation jackpot. America exists by design . . . divine design . . . and American patriots intuitively know that how we are acting is not who we really are.

At some point, what I present will challenge a tradition within your belief system; maybe even one that you are quite fond of. In my years of researching this subject, I have been forced to challenge some of my own Christian assumptions along the way. When I would come to a crossroads challenging a concept near and dear to my heart, I was faced with a choice. Either I permit the Word of God and history to speak for itself and change my false assumptions, or I cling to them and attempt to reshape the Word and history into a mold of my own liking. I chose the former, and I hope you will do the same. My sincerest hope is that you will simply allow the Word of God to speak for itself, and let it be the deciding factor. Do not allow a preconceived idea to take root and get in the way of truth, for that is precisely what blinded the Pharisee's eyes to the One who stood before them and walked their streets.

You will also be challenged to think. Genuine thinking and reason are required to demystify the scripture, and being spiritual does not mean being mystical. The events of the Bible are not mysterious and paranormal as often presented. The biggest challenge for the student when reading the symbolism in prophecy is to normalize it so it can be understood for what it is. The events foretold by the prophets will appear to be the natural consequences of cause and effect as they unfold. This is precisely why so many people will refuse to acknowledge the hand of God at work in these events, and consequently they will not repent. So do not settle for the theater of the absurd when it comes to interpreting dramatic references in scripture. Visions of a crazed antichrist foaming at the mouth and riding a pig into a rebuilt temple may make for great theater, and even sell a lot of books. It gets even better when his horns start to sprout and his head starts spinning around 360 degrees. It's highly entertaining to imagine these images as taking place, but you can be very entertained and yet very blind. The key to understanding the mysteries of scripture is to normalize it rather than further dramatize it.

This book will help you do just that. This book is a primer to help you understand who America is in the Bible. It is said that truth is stranger than fiction, and this book will bear that out. Once you read it, understand it, and embrace the implications, it will cause you to lose sleep. And that's exactly what I want from you the reader. That is the cost of vigilance, and 20-20 vision is necessary if you wish to stand in defense of our nation. Jesus instructed us to "_watch and pray_" during these days, and that requires eyes that see and ears that hear. This book will help tune your understanding, and it will impact every corner of your life. And if you absorb the information, you will be stirred to action.

This book is not offered up for entertainment. It is offered in defense of a nation . . . The United States of America. May God bless this nation once again, and may we learn what it means to be "one nation under God". Let the journey begin!

CHAPTER 1

Keys To Unlocking The Bible

Let's begin by repeating the two key principles brought out in the Forward. They bear repeating because they are foundational to help us strip back the layers of the onion and discover who we are. They are as follows:

1. All people groups have existed from the time of Shem, Ham, and Japheth.

2. Behavior is not the key ingredient in determining core identity.

Consider for a moment the first principle. Shem, Ham and Japheth were Noah's sons. And as survivors of the great flood, EVERY people group of the earth comes from them. As you read this, YOU are a Shemite . . . a Hamite . . . or a Japhethite. You must be from one of these three families.

Due to the ebb and flow of time, migration, and growth, these people groups have existed in either a scattered state or a gathered state. It all was dependent on the situation they faced at the time. But regardless of their global position or coalescence, they (we) have been in existence. So the name of America may not be in the Bible, and our borders may be a thing of modern history, but the people group responsible for our prevailing culture is not new. We have been in scripture since the beginning of time, and God has been speaking to us since Genesis. All throughout scripture, God addresses the various people groups with their ancestral names, not with the names of the borders they now occupy. Understanding this will help you broaden your vision, and help you find the truth of who America is.

The second consideration is equally true, and bears repeating . . . and repeating . . . and repeating. Behavior is not the key ingredient in determining core identity. You are who you are, regardless of how you are behaving. As a nation, America was not birthed in the courts of Heaven one moment, only to become Mystery Babylon (the great whore) the next moment. That thinking does not hold water, because we are who we are. It is all about our DNA.

This is how the Bible addresses people groups, and our thinking needs to flow through this filter. We often come to wrong conclusions because we use the wrong filter. If the water is muddy, the problem is not with the conclusions. The problem is with the filter, and all we have to do is change the filter so things will clear up.

So is America in the Bible? A lot of Bible scholars say "no", but they arrive at that conclusion by ignoring the two principles above. In all honesty, that conclusion does not make any sense. To illustrate this, let's examine a passage of scripture that the global community will soon experience, and we will use it as a launching pad to frame our thoughts from here forward.

The passage is *Ezekiel 38 & 39*, which is a detailed analysis of the next global conflict that is soon to arise. The events contained herein will change the political landscape of the world as we know it today. And since America is presently the global leader of the free world, we must factor in to *Ezekiel 38 & 39* somewhere. As we read it, we'll examine who the players are, and if you don't understand as you read it through, that's OK; I will spend considerable time explaining from here forward. For now, let's familiarize ourselves with the text of this passage.

Ezekiel 38:

> *1 - And the word of the LORD came unto me, saying,*

> *2 - Son of man, set thy face against Gog, the land of Magog, the chief prince of Meshech and Tubal, and prophesy against him,*

3 - And say, Thus saith the LORD GOD; Behold, I am against thee, O Gog, the chief prince of Meshech and Tubal:

4 - And I will turn thee back, and put hooks into thy jaws, and I will bring thee forth, and all thine army, horses and horsemen, all of them clothed with all sorts of armour, even a great company with bucklers and shields, all of them handling swords:

5 - Persia, Ethiopia, and Libya with them; all of them with shield and helmet:

6 - Gomer, and all his bands; the house of Togarmah of the north quarters, and all his bands: and many people with thee.

7 - Be thou prepared, and prepare for thyself, thou, and all thy company that are assembled unto thee, and be thou a guard unto them.

8 - After many days thou shalt be visited: in the latter years thou shalt come into the land that is brought back from the sword, and is gathered out of many people, against the mountains of Israel, which have been always waste: but it is brought forth out of the nations, and they shall dwell safely all of them.

9 - Thou shalt ascend and come like a storm, thou shalt be like a cloud to cover the land, thou, and all thy bands, and many people with thee.

10 - Thus saith the LORD GOD; It shall also come to pass, that at the same time shall things come into thy mind, and thou shalt think an evil thought:

11 - And thou shalt say, I will go up to the land of unwalled villages; I will go to them that are at rest, that dwell safely, all of them dwelling without walls, and having neither bars nor gates,

12 - To take a spoil, and to take a prey; to turn thine hand upon the desolate places that are now inhabited, and upon the people that are gathered out of the nations, which have gotten cattle and goods, that dwell in the midst of the land.

13 - Sheba, and Dedan, and the merchants of Tarshish, with all the young lions thereof, shall say unto thee, Art thou come to take a spoil? hast thou gathered thy company to take a prey? to carry away silver and gold, to take away cattle and goods, to take a great spoil?

14 - Therefore, son of man, prophesy and say unto Gog, Thus saith the LORD GOD; In that day when my people of Israel dwelleth safely, shalt thou not know it?

15 - And thou shalt come from thy place out of the north parts, thou, and many people with thee, all of them riding upon horses, a great company, and a mighty army:

16 - And thou shalt come up against my people of Israel, as a cloud to cover the land; it shall be in the latter days, and I will bring thee against my land, that the heathen may know me, when I shall be sanctified in thee, O Gog, before their eyes.

17 - Thus saith the LORD GOD; Art thou he of whom I have spoken in old time by my servants the prophets of Israel, which prophesied in those days many years that I would bring thee against them?

18 - And it shall come to pass at the same time when Gog shall come against the land of Israel, saith the LORD GOD, that my fury shall come up in my face.

19 - For in my jealousy and in the fire of my wrath have I spoken, Surely in that day there shall be a great shaking in the land of Israel;

20 - So that the fishes of the sea, and the fowls of the heaven, and the Beasts of the field, and all creeping things that creep upon the earth, and all the men that are upon the face of the earth, shall shake at my presence, and the mountains shall be thrown down, and the steep places shall fall, and every wall shall fall to the ground.

21 - And I will call for a sword against him throughout all my mountains, saith the LORD GOD: every man's sword shall be against his brother.

22 - And I will plead against him with pestilence and with blood; and I will rain upon him, and upon his bands, and upon the many people that are with him, an overflowing rain, and great hailstones, fire, and brimstone.

23 - Thus will I magnify myself, and sanctify myself; and I will be known in the eyes of many nations, and they shall know that I am the LORD.

Ezekiel 39:

1 - Therefore, thou son of man, prophesy against Gog, and say, Thus saith the LORD GOD; Behold, I am against thee, O Gog, the chief prince of Meshech and Tubal:

2 - And I will turn thee back, and leave but the sixth part of thee, and will cause thee to come up from the north parts, and will bring thee upon the mountains of Israel:

3 - And I will smite thy bow out of thy left hand, and will cause thine arrows to fall out of thy right hand.

4 - Thou shalt fall upon the mountains of Israel, thou, and all thy bands, and the people that is with thee: I will give thee unto the ravenous birds of every sort, and to the Beasts of the field to be devoured.

5 - Thou shalt fall upon the open field: for I have spoken it, saith the LORD GOD.

6 - And I will send a fire on Magog, and among them that dwell carelessly in the isles: and they shall know that I am the LORD.

7 - So will I make my holy name known in the midst of my people Israel; and I will not let them pollute my holy name any more: and the heathen shall know that I am the LORD, the Holy One in Israel.

8 - Behold, it is come, and it is done, saith the LORD GOD; this is the day whereof I have spoken.

9 - And they that dwell in the cities of Israel shall go forth, and shall set on fire and burn the weapons, both the shields and the bucklers, the bows and the arrows, and the handstaves, and the spears, and they shall burn them with fire seven years:

10 - So that they shall take no wood out of the field, neither cut down any out of the forests; for they shall burn the weapons with fire: and they shall spoil those that spoiled them, and rob those that robbed them, saith the LORD GOD.

11 - And it shall come to pass in that day, that I will give unto Gog a place there of graves in Israel, the valley of the passengers on the east of the sea: and it shall stop the noses of the passengers: and there shall they bury Gog and all his multitude: and they shall call it The valley of Hamongog.

12 - And seven months shall the house of Israel be burying of them, that they may cleanse the land.

13 - Yea, all the people of the land shall bury them; and it shall be to them a renown the day that I shall be glorified, saith the LORD GOD.

14 - And they shall sever out men of continual employment, passing through the land to bury with the passengers those that remain upon the face of the earth, to cleanse it: after the end of seven months shall they search.

15 - And the passengers that pass through the land, when any seeth a man's bone, then shall he set up a sign by it, till the buriers have buried it in the valley of Hamongog.

16 - And also the name of the city shall be Hamonah. Thus shall they cleanse the land.

17 - And, thou son of man, thus saith the LORD GOD; Speak unto every feathered fowl, and to every Beast of the field, Assemble yourselves, and come; gather yourselves on every side to my sacrifice that I do sacrifice for you, even a great sacrifice upon the mountains of Israel, that ye may eat flesh, and drink blood.

18 - Ye shall eat the flesh of the mighty, and drink the blood of the princes of the earth, of rams, of lambs, and of goats, of bullocks, all of them fatlings of Bashan.

19 - And ye shall eat fat till ye be full, and drink blood till ye be drunken, of my sacrifice which I have sacrificed for you.

20 - Thus ye shall be filled at my table with horses and chariots, with mighty men, and with all men of war, saith the LORD GOD.

21 - And I will set my glory among the heathen, and all the heathen shall see my judgment that I have executed, and my hand that I have laid upon them.

22 - So the house of Israel shall know that I am the LORD their God from that day and forward.

23 - And the heathen shall know that the house of Israel went into captivity for their iniquity: because they trespassed against me, therefore hid I my face from them, and gave them into the hand of their enemies: so fell they all by the sword.

24 - According to their uncleanness and according to their transgressions have I done unto them, and hid my face from them.

25 - Therefore thus saith the LORD GOD; Now will I bring again the captivity of Jacob, and have mercy upon the whole house of Israel, and will be jealous for my holy name;

26 - After that they have borne their shame, and all their trespasses whereby they have trespassed against me, when they dwelt safely in their land, and none made them afraid.

27 - When I have brought them again from the people, and gathered them out of their enemies' lands, and am sanctified in them in the sight of many nations;

28 - Then shall they know that I am the LORD their God, which caused them to be led into captivity among the heathen: but I have gathered them unto their own land, and have left none of them any more there.

29 - Neither will I hide my face any more from them: for I have poured out my spirit upon the house of Israel, saith the LORD GOD.

Understand that this was penned sometime around 580 BC, and the names used to describe various nations don't appear as such on our maps today. That's because Ezekiel referred to them by their ancient people-group names, not by their present-day national names. Ezekiel had no way of knowing what these nations would be called some 2,500 years into the future, so he referred to them with their names as they existed at that time. A lot can change over 2,500 years, including national names.

However, the nations named as Gog, Magog, Persia, etc. must be in existence today since *Ezekiel 38:8* pins the fulfillment of this passage to the "latter years" or last days. My immediate conclusion is that these nations exist today, but they must exist under different names. There is no getting around their existence or their apparent name changes. As an example, Gog is nowhere to be found on a map with that name, but if the Bible is true (which it is), Gog must exist today as a superpower capable of waging this war and equipping this alliance. Simply put, Gog is the people group as it existed then, but the people group is probably known today by a modern national name defining its existence as something other than Gog. If the truth be told, it's probably that way for every other player in this passage of scripture. I want to know who they are! Let's begin with the trouble makers.

First and foremost is Gog. He is named as the chief prince of Meshech, which the New American Standard Bible defines as Rosh. He is also the kingpin over a place called Tubal. In the day of Ezekiel's writings, Rosh, Meshech and Tubal were regions or cities north of the Black Sea and Caspian Sea, and east of modern-day Finland. Since these regions and cities have not moved, it doesn't take long to understand that Gog is Russia. There are some today who believe Gog may be Turkey, but we'll address that in a few moments and show how that cannot be. It is important to note however that Gog is not acting alone. He is the head (or mastermind) of an alliance which is of similar thinking. His alliance is all operating with one mind in this endeavor.

Added to Gog is Persia, which is modern-day Iran. The Persian Empire is easy to trace, and the Iranian people know that they are Persian. Persia in 580 B.C. is Iran today. Again, we see an ancient name used for a modern people group known with a different national name. The same holds true for the other nations in this alliance as well. Ethiopia then was the region surrounding modern-day Sudan and Ethiopia. Libya then consisted of much of the modern North African countries.

Gomer, Togarmah and Magog are related, and they point to a different people in a different geographical region. These people are all descendants of Japheth. The descendants of Japheth migrated into the area known today as China, Mongolia, Vietnam, etc.. The people of oriental descent have descended from Japheth. Magog in that day was also identified as a barbaric northern nation to the east of the Caspian Sea. Once again it's not hard to see that China factors into this alliance, and Ezekiel identified them by their names as they existed 2,500 years ago. In short, this is a Russian / Chinese / Muslim alliance, and their alliance is formed to overtake one group of people: The House of Israel.

When you think of such an alliance, each player brings something to the table that is needed for this onslaught. Russia brings weaponry and technology to the table. China brings sheer man power into the mix. With an immediate capability for a 100-million man army, and a resource pool of one billion people, China is a formidable foe for any nation even if their only weapons are Billy Clubs. Finally, there's the Islamic faction added to this. Islam brings hatred for anything it defines as the infidel, and combined this is an unholy alliance formed to oppose God's plan for the House of Israel. It is a toxic brew hell-bent on their destruction.

Now that we have a bird's eye view of this event, one compelling question comes to mind; how or where does America fit into this scenario? Does it seem strange to anyone that America appears to be gone or not interested in this major attack on the House of Israel? If America is gone, where did we go? If we are not interested in this, when did we become so ambivalent to the aspirations of a Communist/Muslim takeover of the world? This position makes absolutely no sense.

Also consider the practical ramifications of _Ezekiel 38:7_. There it states that Gog (Russia) is commissioned to act as a guardian over the other nations that are joined to her, and that includes Iran. If you think this alliance is a conglomerate of strange bed fellows, just follow the voting on the UN Security Council when these nations are involved. Even now, Russia, China and Iran stand together. When the United States wants to step in to stop Iran from becoming a nuclear power, Russia and China veto our proposed sanctions. The nation of Turkey is not the big dog behind Iran, and this is why they cannot be Gog. Turkey may be quietly complicit in Iran's affairs, but Russia is clearly the strength behind the actions of Iran. Russia is the big dog allowing the little dog of Iran to bark. The alliance exists just as God said it would some 2,500 years ago, so if the United States rattles its sabers against a nuclear Iran, wouldn't Russia consider that an act of war? If they are the guardian over Iran, one would certainly think so, and if that's the case then America is neck-deep in this chapter in some way. Where are we?

But for now, let's put first things first. Before we seek to uncover America's involvement, we must deal with the nation being attacked; the House of Israel. In every case, we have seen that the ancient name used in _Ezekiel 38_ does not correlate to the modern name of the players. Is the House of Israel of 2,500 years ago the Jewish State of Israel as seen on a map today? Let's find out.

Our study of Israel begins in the book of Genesis. A very condensed story of Israel's existence goes something like this: Abraham begat Isaac . . . Isaac begat Jacob . . . Jacob's name was changed to Israel . . . and that's where his name first appears. As a person, Israel is far from perfect, but He is chosen by God to raise up a covenant people. With the help of 2 wives,

2 concubines, and 1 adoption, Israel then produces the lineage of sons as illustrated below.

Through Leah (wife #1), Israel has the sons:

- Reuben
- Simeon
- Levi
- Judah
- Issachar
- Zebulun

Through Rachel (wife #2), the sons:

- Joseph
- Benjamin

Through Bilah (Concubine), the sons:

- Dan
- Naphtali

Through Zilpah (Concubine), the sons:

- Gad
- Asher

Through adoption, the sons:

- Manasseh
- Ephraim

These are the sons of Israel arranged by mother and birth order. They became the many nations promised to Abraham in *Genesis 17*, and detailed in *Genesis 49*. According to *Genesis 49:1*, these nations of Israel must be in existence in the last days, and they are fulfilling today what was decreed over them in *Genesis 49*. You may want to take some time and acquaint yourself with these passages of scripture to know what God has decreed over all these sons of Israel. At this point in our study, it is a pretty safe assumption to think that all or some of them comprise the House of Israel as outlined in *Ezekiel 38*. But I don't want to settle for assumptions, so moving forward from here I will put that assumption to the test.

Bear in mind that as God's covenant people, the tribes of Israel were all obligated to build their national life around God, the laws of Moses, and eventually Jesus Christ. In short, they were commissioned by God to be one nation under God. Anything less than that on their part obligated God to judgment on His part. He may be a loving God, but He is also a jealous God.

As you read the prophets throughout scripture, one of the tribes of Israel stands head-and-shoulders above all the others; the tribe of Ephraim originating from the second son of Joseph. Ephraim was one of the adopted sons, and you can reference *Genesis 48* for the details of his adoption by Israel. He is the last of the sons to directly carry the name of Israel. Ephraim would become very prominent, and the prophets have a lot to say about him. Hosea especially speaks a lot about Ephraim and his role in the tribes of Israel. It is due in large part to the materialistic blessings Ephraim received as part of the birthright blessing. The prophets also have a lot to say about an entity known as the House of Israel, over which the tribe of Ephraim became the administrative head.

Here now is where things get tricky if you SKIM . . . rather than STUDY . . . the Word of God: This united kingdom of Israel, comprised of all the sons and their tribes, is NOT the House of Israel as detailed throughout scripture. That title is reserved for a narrower people group. Let me explain.

For hundreds of years spanning from Genesis into 1 Kings, the tribes would remain together and be one united kingdom. I like to refer to them as the UK of I, or the United Kingdom of Israel. However, their domestic tranquility is apparently strained under King Solomon due to taxation, and things come to a boiling point in *1 Kings 11&12*. There we find out what happens to the united kingdom of Israel to bring it to a place of division.

Under Solomon, taxes were high. And the people grew tired of it. They always do when the government wants more than its fair share, which is usually far less than what government thinks. So when Solomon passed on, and his son Rehoboam became king over all the tribes of Israel, the people petitioned him to lower the tax burdens that had been placed on them. Unfortunately for the United Kingdom of Israel, Rehoboam's government was not one of the people, by the people, or for the people. It was for himself, and the people were his subjects. Rehoboam ended up doing the opposite of what the people wanted, and he raised taxes. Or shall I say that he promised to raise taxes, but his IRS agents were never able to collect. The people upended his plan with what I call the tea party of 928 BC, and 10 of the colonies declared their independence from the mother country. Essentially they told king Rehoboam that he could take his increased taxation and take a hike, and they served him notice that they were no longer under his thumb. The secession was under way. This resulted in a divided kingdom, and the colonial alliances fell into place as follows:

The House of Israel consisted of 10 colonies:

- Joseph (who eventually become the dual tribe of Ephraim and Manasseh)
- Reuben
- Simeon
- Levi
- Issachar
- Zebulun
- Gad
- Asher
- Dan
- Naphtali

As noted, the colony of Joseph was eventually absorbed by the tribes of his sons; Ephraim and Manasseh. Ephraim eventually became the administrative head over the entire 10-tribed kingdom.

The House of Judah, led by the tribe of Judah, consisted of two colonies and a smattering of a third:

- Judah
- Benjamin
- Some Levites

Because of heavy taxation by the monarchy, the colonies of Israel divided into two distinct national entities that are mentioned throughout scripture. One is known as the House of Israel . . . and it consists of ten primary colonies. It would eventually be led by the colony of Ephraim which was known for having the Midas touch. The other national entity to emerge from the split is the House of Judah . . . and it consists of two primary colonies. It was led by the colony of Judah which was known for having the royal lineage. One got the money, the other got the crown.

It's important to understand that the House of Israel was birthed by a tea-party-tax-revolt and a declaration of independence! Were it not for these events, the House of Israel would not exist. If you read the account on your own, you will find that those dedicated to a united kingdom declared war on the secessionists for their actions. But God ruled on the side of the House of Israel, and the kingdom was divided from that point forward. In essence, the secessionists prevailed, and a new nation was born. That nation was known in scripture to be the House of Israel, and it did not include the colonies of Judah and Benjamin.

It is difficult to read the Old Testament prophets without seeing them address one of these two people groups. One minute they are writing to the House of Judah. The next chapter, they are writing to the House of Israel. The reason is simple; it is because they are two distinct people groups. They are so different that they even migrated to completely different geographical regions. The House of Israel was taken captive by the Assyrians around 720 BC, and eventually because of migration and exploration, they left the regions of Palestine completely.

A quick study of _Hosea 1_ also reveals what happened as the House of Israel scattered and left the area. They began to lose an understanding of their heritage. They were still the House of Israel, but they quickly fell into idolatry and globalist thinking, and they forgot who they were. They were one nation under God, but they no longer cared for the obligations associated with that title. As detailed in _Hosea 1:10_, they would eventually be known by another name, yet God would always know them to be the House of Israel. And as seen in *Ezekiel 38*, they exist in living color in the last days! When you read the account of their national status, they are wealthy, dwelling in peace, living without bars or gates, and they are afraid of nobody. This is the House of Israel that Russia, China, and Islam want to overthrow. And the House of Israel *does not know who they are* in God's eyes. For now, let's return to understanding the distinction between the two houses; the House of Israel and the House of Judah. The ramifications have great consequence regarding our understanding of God's Word, and where events will occur as prophesied.

When the House of Israel was led away from the regions of Palestine, the House of Judah remained behind; even after a brief period of captivity in Babylon. As these brother nations separated further and further apart, God's Word was still true to each of them despite their behavior. Sometimes their behavior was good. Most of the time it was not. But God's goodness to them was not based on their nature; it was based on God's nature. All of the promises He had made would still be fulfilled in one or both of these kingdoms, even when they walked in rebellion to God. Biblical history shows that they eventually came to take on completely different attributes. A quick glance at the following list shows how various aspects of God's promises were fulfilled in each national entity.

Characteristics of the House of Judah:

- Judah would take on a nickname; that being "Jew". This is merely a contraction of Judah.
- Judah would possess Palestine.
- Judah would speak the original Hebrew tongue.
- Judah would be a remnant of people, or few in number.
- Judah would be well known, and not detached from their heritage like the House of Israel.
- Judah would be a singular nation.
- Judah (through the Lion of the tribe of Judah) would possess the royalty blessing . . . and this entitled them to the lineage of the Messiah.

But what about the House of Israel? Let's take a look. These are the characteristics of the House of Israel:

- Israel would have a name change.
- Israel would acquire their own land separate from Palestine.
- Israel would speak a new language.
- Israel would be as the sands of the sea in multitude.
- Israel would be lost to their heritage
- Israel would become a company or commonwealth of nations.
- Israel (through Ephraim) would possess the birthright blessing . . . and this entitled them to great materialistic wealth.

There is a lot of distinction between the two Kingdoms!

For now, let's focus on one key difference; that being their name. Hosea has told us that the House of Israel would lose the understanding of their identity, and take on a new name. The House of Judah, however, would not, and they would adopt a nickname consistent with their colonial name. The nickname is "Jew", which is short for Judah. EVERY reference in scripture to the phrase "Jew", "Jews", or "Jewish" is a reference to either the colony or the Kingdom of Judah. To carry the title of "Jew", you had to be connected to the House of Judah. Some examples include Jesus, Paul, and Daniel. Jesus was of the tribe of Judah, and therefore a Jew. The same holds true for Daniel. Paul was a Benjaminite, but since Benjamin sided with the House of Judah, they too took on the nickname of "Jew". This is why Paul refers to himself as such. It's because he fulfilled the requirements to bear that nickname.

If you consider the entire conglomerate of Israel, which is all the colonies combined, the Jewish portion of Israel is quite small. It is the House of Judah, and they essentially are a state within the greater nation of Israel. But the Jews are not the entire nation of Israel. Think of it this way; Colorado is a State, but it is not the entire nation. It is just one piece of the nation, and that's how the Jewish piece looks when you're talking about Israel as a whole. All Coloradoans are American, but not all Americans are Coloradoans. In like manner, all Jews are Israelites, but not all Israelites are Jews. This is why Ephraim or ANY of the colonies who lined up with the House of Israel would never be called Jewish. They are Israelites . . . detached from their heritage . . . but they do not qualify to call themselves Jewish. In short, the House of Israel is not the Jewish people! The Jewish state of Israel as it is appropriately named is the House of Judah in scripture. The House of Israel is a national entity completely distinct from the Jewish people. Are they related? Yes. Are they identical? No. This is clearly outlined in scripture when the nickname "Jew" first begins to show up. The first time it is used is in *2 Kings 16:6*; and there we see that Israel is fighting the "Jews". It is obvious that they are distinct people groups. Without belaboring the point, the titles of "Israel" and "Jew" are not synonymous, and they do not refer to the same people group. If that is the case, we need to zero in on the House of Israel and see what we can learn about them.

Due to Ephraim's blessing in *Genesis 48* the House of Israel would have possession of the materialistic blessing and would be destined to owning the wealth of the world. That would serve to draw the rest of the world to her and garner one of two responses from the global community; either they would want to be part of Ephraim, or they would be jealous and want to destroy her. As a result, the House of Israel would become a melting pot of people with great wealth, and on the other hand a major threat to other nations who don't like her strength and dominance.

Look for a moment at God's promise to Joseph, who was the father of Ephraim. It is found in *Deuteronomy 33:13-17*, and it reads as follows:

> *13 - And of Joseph he said, Blessed of the LORD be his land, for the precious things of heaven, for the dew, and for the deep that coucheth beneath,*

> *14 - And for the precious fruits brought forth by the sun, and for the precious things put forth by the moon,*

> *15 - And for the chief things of the ancient mountains, and for the precious things of the lasting hills,*

> *16 - And for the precious things of the earth and fullness thereof, and for the good will of him that dwelt in the bush: let the blessing come*

upon the head of Joseph, and upon the top of the head of him that was separated from his brethren.

17 - His glory is like the firstling of his bullock, and his horns are like the horns of unicorns: with them he shall push the people together to the ends of the earth: and they are the ten thousands of Ephraim, and they are the thousands of Manasseh.

Joseph is blessed! That is the blessing carried by Ephraim and Manasseh, and in addition to that Ephraim got the greater blessing from Israel himself in *Genesis 48*. Ephraim carries a double blessing, which is what his name means. Ephraim translated means "double fruit", and he is shown to be the wealthy one among all the tribes. No wonder he would become the administrative head over the House of Israel.

Of specific interest in this promise is *Deuteronomy 33:17* where God declares that Ephraim and Manasseh will push the people to the ends of the earth. This speaks of colonialism and expansion, well beyond the borders of Palestine. Bear in mind that Israel was promised NOT ONLY Palestine; they were also promised territories to the north, south, east and west. Speaking to Israel in *Genesis 28:14*, God says *"And thy seed shall be as the dust of the earth, and thou shalt spread abroad to the west, and to the east, and to the north, and to the south: and in thee and in thy seed shall all the families of the earth be blessed"*. Many people wrongly assume that Palestine is the ONLY land promised to Israel, but God promised much more to them than that. As seen in *Deuteronomy 33:17*, their spreading abroad would take them to the "ends" of the earth, and it also infers that Ephraim will possess great wealth and prosperity. I wonder where all of these descriptions converge?

When I was growing up in church, I often heard Missionaries speak of their endeavors in other parts of the world. In my mind, I always imagined the remote regions of Asia or Africa to be the ends of the earth. After all, measuring outward from Colorado, Zimbabwe is pretty far away. From my perspective, that is the end of the earth because of where my starting point is. My frame of reference begins in Colorado, and the end of the earth is the furthest possible spot from where I am standing.

The only problem with that mental picture is that God did not make these promises to Ephraim and Manasseh in Colorado; He made these promises in proximity to Palestine. That is the real starting point, and if you want the right perspective on where God ordained Ephraim to go, you have to measure around the globe using Palestine as the starting point; not Colorado. So where might the ends of the earth be if Palestine is the starting point of your measurement? The furthest land mass from Palestine is the West Coast of what is known today as the United States. Today that's called California, Hawaii, and Alaska! But in _Deuteronomy_, God was calling that the ends of the earth, and that's where He was telling Joseph that his sons would go. They would literally colonize all the way around the globe to the other side of the earth, and carry with them the promise of great wealth.

Their migration did not happen overnight, but it did happen. By the time of Jeremiah's death, the House of Israel was long gone from the regions of Palestine, and they were losing their identity. While the House of Judah had claimed a nickname . . . that of "Jew" . . . the House of Israel would soon lay claim to a new nickname of its own. As the House of Israel, they were rightfully known as Isaac's sons . . . but like Judah, they too would drop a few letters from their title. "Isaac's sons" would eventually become "'saac's sons", and it's not hard to see how that could become "Saxons" when spoken quickly. These "'saac's sons" were moving (probably unknowingly) towards their promised possession in the uttermost part of the earth with a completely new ethnic name. It was the House of Israel . . . with a new name . . . migrating to a new location. The House of Israel led by Ephraim to the ends of the earth.

This explains why Jeremiah's tomb is in Ireland, which is a study in and of itself as to how he got there. Google it if you want to see it.

This explains why the Scottish Declaration of Independence, penned in 1218, refers to the Scottish people as the "_outgoings of the house of Israel_". Google it also if you want to see it. The Scottish people literally descended from the House of Israel, and this migrating kingdom left some of its people in Scotland as they continued their push to the uttermost part of the earth.

This is why people of Scandinavian descent have surnames such as Jacobson, Isaacson, and Abrahamson.

If the Jews, who still spoke the Hebrew language, referred to these covenant people, they would call them the beriyth-ish. The Hebrew word "beriyth" means covenant, and the Hebrew word "ish" means man. A beriyth-ish was literally a "covenant man", and it's not hard to see how the beriyth-ish would eventually become known as the British.

Regarding their new language, the prophet Isaiah addresses Ephraim and the House of Israel this way: *Isaiah 28:11 - For with stammering lips and another tongue will he speak to this people*. The LORD is not speaking to the Jewish portion of Israel in this passage, He is speaking specifically to Ephraim and the House of Israel. On the surface that scripture may not sound like much, but consider what it says in the Hebrew tongue in which Isaiah writes it. The Hebrew word for "stammering" is translated as "gael". And as we have already learned, the Hebrew word for man is "ish". So for a Jew to speak in Hebrew of Ephraim's new language, he would say that God was going to speak to Ephraim in "gael". As a result, the men of Ephraim would rightfully be known as "gael-ish" or "stammering lipped men". An "gaelish" is easily seen now as "English".

And finally, if the House of Israel was anything like Ephraim's father (Joseph) in Egypt, they would feed the world and be its savior in the final resting place of blessing that God had for him in the ends of the earth. People would gather to Ephraim and the House of Israel as a result, and the nation would become a melting pot of many nations.

So today, if you can find:

- One nation under God . . .
- A national conglomeration of all the colonies of Israel . . .
- Saxon ('saac's sons) in origin . . . yet joined by other nations . . .
- An an-gael-ish (English) speaking people . . .
- A nation which has accumulated wealth . . .
- A nation who is feeding the world and being a blessing . . .
- A nation who possesses land holdings half-way around the world from Palestine . . .

Then THAT is the House of Israel, and you have just found the nation that Russia/China/Islam invades (much to its surprise) in _Ezekiel 38 & 39_. The House of Israel is caught completely by surprise because they are powerful, wealthy, dwelling in peace, dwelling without bars or gates, and nobody makes them afraid. But to this tyrannical alliance arrayed against them, the House of Israel has something they want. They have the goods. Cattle, spoil and goods is how it is referred to in _Ezekiel 38_. They are the breadbasket of the world, and Gog wants it for himself. To this alliance, the House of Israel is enemy number one and they must be removed from the global scene if they want to impose their agenda of tyranny upon the world.

Ezekiel understood that the Kingdom names of the House of Judah and the House of Israel were NOT synonymous, and he was referring specifically to the House of Israel. Apparently he had never seen it before, which is probably why he went to such lengths to explain it in detail. Ezekiel was witness to what the House of Israel would look like in the last days, and also witness to the other nations wanting to destroy her. Perhaps you would do well to reread _Ezekiel 38 & 39_ and look at it a little more closely. It is coming soon to a street corner near you.

We can now answer the questions that were unanswered at the start of our chapter. Who is this House of Israel and how does America fit into the events of _Ezekiel 38_? Like all the other nations in that chapter, the House of Israel was being called by their ancient name, and they are in existence today under a completely different name. The House of Israel is the United States of America.

Once you understand the division of the two houses, the Bible becomes much more intelligible. And what I'm writing of is nothing new. It's actually quite old. Google it if you want to see it. Wikipedia has a virtual who's who of notable men and movements who espoused these truths. One of them is Charles Adelle Lewis Totten, who was the Professor of Military Science and Tactics at Yale University (1851-1908). He had this to say about these facts: _"I can never be too thankful to the Almighty that in my youth he used the late Professor Wilson to show me the difference between the two houses. The very understanding of this difference is the KEY by which almost the entire Bible becomes intelligible, and I cannot state too strongly_ *that the man who has not yet seen that Israel of the scripture is totally distinct from the Jewish people, is yet in the very infancy, the mere alphabet of Biblical study, and that to this day the meaning of seven-eighths of the Bible is shut to his understanding."*

As we conclude this chapter, consider this verse; *Ezekiel 38:17 - Thus saith the LORD GOD; Art thou he (Gog) of whom I have spoken in old time by my servants the prophets of Israel . . . which prophesied in those days . . . many years . . . that I would bring thee against them?* Ezekiel presents this as a rhetorical question which is really just a statement of fact. If we remove the question mark and frame it as a statement, it would sound like this: *Thus saith the LORD GOD; thou (Gog) art he of whom I have spoken in old time by my servants the prophets of Israel . . . which prophesied in those days . . . many years . . . that I would bring thee against them.* This verse is important because through it we understand that God has revealed this same event to other prophets. And if that's the case, they must have written about it as well. If we can find their writings of this same event, we can assemble a larger picture of what America will soon face and how we can stand in her defense. Buckle up; it's going to be a fun ride!

CHAPTER 2

The Big Picture

It has been my experience that studies of a similar nature typically end where I left off in chapter one. I own a sizeable collection of books that bring the student to understand that America is the House of Israel, and then they end. At best they take the student through *Ezekiel 38*, and thus end their book, study, or lecture. However, I intend to use the conclusions from chapter one as our starting point. Now that we know who America is in the Bible, we want to build that forward and paint a much broader picture of how everything weaves together. The scripture has a lot to say about the House of Israel, and the implications are enormous. It promises to be an exciting ride as we move forward, and by the end of this book you will have an understanding of what is playing out in the headlines before our very eyes.

If we expect to uncover the truth, our approach to scripture should be as follows; ANY New Testament prophets or prophecies MUST be in alignment with everything detailed in the Old Testament. I have read the Bible from cover to cover, and nowhere have I found the word "oops". In either the Greek or the Hebrew. We cannot detach the New from the Old and expect to understand Bible prophecy. It takes a complete Bible to make a complete Christian, and for this reason we want to use the whole text in our study. Jesus is not schizophrenic, and He doesn't start one story only to throw it away in favor of a new one. He builds line upon line, precept upon precept, here a little and there a little. The foundation remains intact as new layers are added to the truth that previous prophets revealed. This is precisely why we did not begin in the New Testament. We had to begin where God began so we could lay the right foundation BEFORE getting to the New Testament. It is the finishing touches on what the prophets before it illustrated in great detail. So if you want to understand the end, you must understand the beginning. To be fractionally off in Genesis is to be miles off in Revelation.

As we move forward through this book, we will show how the last day system of evil intends to propagate and control humanity, and how the House of Israel and House of Judah will be affected by it. This system of evil is called a "Beast" system in the Bible, and many associate it with such labels as "antichrist". We also intend to show you some compelling trigger points that bring the conflict to a head, and these are the things to watch for. This will all be discussed in great detail in the chapters ahead. As an appetizer I'll tell you now that the Beast system has two primary enemies which it utterly hates. Two "houses" if you will, and we will show you who they are. Both appear in the New Testament in The Revelation, and in the Old Testament which is the foundation of The Revelation. Since the prophets must agree, scripture will be used to interpret scripture as we handle things hard to understand. You will see that the prophets are saying the same things, but with different details and labels specific to the revelation they receive from God. To further hone your thinking along these lines, consider that there are only two nations on earth today that have been built upon the principles of scripture. One is still looking for the Messiah. This is the Jewish State of Israel, which we know as the House of Judah. The other has built their nation upon the Messiah. This is the United States of America, which we now know as the House of Israel. Neither one is complete in how they've developed the rule of law in their society. The House of Judah focuses on the first five books of the Old Testament, and ignores the rest. The House of Israel focuses on the first five books of the New Testament, and increasingly ignores the rest. We are both blinded in part to the whole of scripture and what God requires of our nations, and since our breakup in *1 Kings 11 & 12*, we are a house divided. This is something which Jesus said cannot stand. We are the only two nations in history BUILT by scripture, yet we both ignore large sections to our peril. Other nations in existence have been introduced to the scripture, but these two nations retained the privilege of building on scripture from the ground up. Could the House of Israel and the House of Judah be the two entities most hated by the Beast system in the last days? Stay tuned.

Before we jump into the substantive issues mentioned above, let's first deal with the issue of time. We need to understand what is happening, but we also need to understand when it will happen. To do that, we must understand time as God created it. We'll begin this leg of our journey with a couple of scriptures. The first is found in *1 John 5*, and it reads as follows:

1 John 5:

> *7 - For there are three that bear record in heaven, the Father, the Word, and the Holy Ghost: and these three are one.*

> *8 - And there are three that bear witness in earth, the Spirit, and the water, and the blood: and these three agree in one.*

God reveals Himself to mankind in some way through these "threes". There are three spiritual expressions which we cannot see (the Father, the Word, the Holy Ghost), and three physical expressions which we can see (Spirit, water, blood). I'll show you how we see them all in a few moments. The overarching question however is this; what does this mean, and what is its relevance to our study? How does it relate to this thing called time? Before I answer, let's read another verse found in *2 Peter*.

2 Peter 3:

> *8 - But, beloved, be not ignorant of this one thing, that one day is with the LORD as a thousand years, and a thousand years as one day.*

In like fashion, we're left wondering what this means. What is its relevance to our study? To answer, let's look at the big picture which I'll refer to as God's redemptive week. We'll work to decipher the big picture as painted by God using the clues given to us in these passages. The following graphic lays it out best, and make sure you study the details of it before reading on.

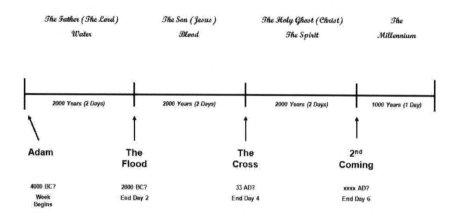

The graphic shows that the LORD has divided the 6,000 years of human history as revealed in scripture into three distinct time periods. I will refer to them as dispensations. Each dispensation consists of equal time lengths of roughly 2,000 years each. None of us were around when these periods of time started or stopped, but with the help of history we draw the conclusion that each dispensation of time was approximately 2,000 years long. Whatever dates we may assign to events for the sake of study need to have question marks behind them rather than exclamation points, for we cannot, with perfect precision, figure out God's timetable. We cannot know the day or the hour of Christ's return, but we can and should know the seasons (*1 Thessalonians 5:1*). We are in the season of the last days, and we know we are close to the end of year number 6,000. The time of Christ's return draws near, as do the events preceding His return.

In total, the time given to human administration over the earth amounts to 6,000 years, and it will be capped off with a 1,000 year period known as the Millennium. During this final 1,000 year period Christ will rule and reign on this earth. It is the Kingdom Age, and it consists of perfected administration over the affairs of man on earth. This is why there is a resurrection at Christ's return. The resurrection is necessary because the Kingdom ON EARTH is the goal. Far too many Christians are consumed with getting out of here, while God is consumed with getting His Kingdom into here. It will be a great day for the saints of old when they once again step foot on this planet to rule and reign with Christ. This is what they long for, and we should make the best of our time allotment on earth while we have it. All total, the cumulative time period is a total of 7,000 years, and there are distinct physical characteristics of each dispensation.

First, there is dispensation #1. It is approximately a 2,000 year period from Adam to the flood. According to *Genesis 2:5-6*, the earth was not watered with rain during this time. It was watered with a mist, also known as dew. This dispensation was marked by dew at the beginning, and continued that way right up to the very end. That is when the earth had an encounter with a magnified expression of dew, and in the Bible it is known as the flood. That is dew on steroids.

As we consider the water marks left on this period of time, a few things of interest stand out. First, we find that the magnified expression (the flood) was largely missed by most until it was too late. Noah only knew of its impending onslaught because of divine revelation, and as he warned the people of it, I'm sure it did not register to them. After all, how can dew drops cause a flood? Dew is all they knew, and to them this was the way it would always be. Until the flood came and caught them by surprise. In spite of Noah warning the people for a century, it snuck up on the masses and they did not see it coming. The second point of interest is this; the magnified expression at the end of the period was much larger than the initial expression at the beginning of and during this period. It was the exclamation point at the end of the sentence. This is pretty easy to understand. For 2,000 years the earth had experienced a baptism of dew, and at the end of that time period it got an immersion that made the precursor pale in comparison. It was the drop vs. the deluge. They are both an expression of H_2O, but they are completely different in scale and size. As we think back now on our scripture in *1 John 5*, from the three that bear witness on earth, this time period was marked by water. God revealed himself as the Father during this time, and He literally baptized the earth with a water baptism. This was the Father's baptism.

Next up is dispensation #2. This is the central dispensation in human history, and it too is approximately a 2,000 year period. It extends roughly from the period after Noah's flood to Calvary. What characterizes this time period, however, is not water; it is blood. Think of how the blood mark was left on this period of time as you read through the scripture. The Abrahamic covenant was sealed with the shedding of blood through circumcision. There is the shedding of blood enduring throughout this dispensation in the form of animal sacrifices. As the children of Israel experienced their deliverance from Egypt, their ultimate form of protection was with the blood placed over the door posts of their homes. At the front end of this time period, the offering of Isaac in sacrifice was a symbolic type of the Father offering up the Son. This dispensation then closes with the promised child Jesus shedding His blood and ushering in a New Covenant.

While it's a different physical expression during this time, it has some striking similarities. First, the magnified expression at the end was largely missed by most, though it happened right in front of them. In this case it wasn't known as the flood; it was known as the cross. In spite of the prophets providing clear and advanced notice of a coming Savior who would give His life, it snuck up on the masses. Jesus even wept over them because they "*knew not the time of their visitation*". Second, this magnified expression was much larger than the initial expression at the beginning of and during this period. Up until the sacrifice of Jesus, the many animal sacrifices could be likened to the dew drops of sacrifice. They were very small in comparison. The offering of Christ, however, was the ultimate sacrifice, the finished work. So if the flood was dew on steroids, the cross was sacrifice on steroids. They were not even on the same playing field. The first is the symbol, and the latter is the fulfillment. And just as with the first dispensation, there would never be another magnified expression of this period. The grand finale was complete, and just as there would be no more flood, neither would there be any more shedding of blood. It was finished, and the exclamation point was placed at the end of this sentence. So of the three that bear witness on earth, this central dispensation of time was marked by the shedding of blood as God revealed Himself through the form of His Son. God literally made provision for mankind to be baptized in the blood of Christ, thus offering salvation to all. This was the Son's baptism.

We come now to the third and present time period, dispensation #3. With the conclusion of Calvary, God had revealed Himself as the Father and the Son to mankind, and had left two physical witnesses of His work, water and blood. There is only one way left to reveal Himself, and that is as the Holy Ghost with a corresponding physical witness. If this dispensation of time holds to the same patterns as displayed in the other ones, we can make some educated assumptions about how it will look towards the end, and what its length of time will be. Generally speaking, this dispensation of time began at Pentecost in *Acts 2*, and will extend up to the second coming of Jesus Christ. If it is consistent with the previous dispensations, this one will also prove to be about 2,000 years in length. We cannot know the exact time period involved, but it will be close to this window of time just as the previous dispensations were. And as stated earlier, since the other two physical expressions of water and blood are already used for other time periods, the only one left is that of the Spirit. How has the Spirit placed His stamp on the earth during our present era? Like the others, it must be visible for all to see, and we want to know what it is.

The initial expression of this Spirit baptism is found in *Acts 2*. It is very important for people to read this passage of scripture because it shows us what the dew drop of the Spirit's expression looks like. This is the symbol. Once we understand that, we can look for the deluge at the end of the time period. In a nutshell, here's what we see in *Acts 2*. There we find a group of redeemed Israelites gathered together in one geographical place, functioning as one unified culture centered on Christ, and they are given other tongues with which to speak. Though these tongues were new, they were universally understood by the multicultural community around them. Shortly thereafter in *Acts 10*, believing gentiles are brought into the same experience and language, and for the first time since the tower of Babel, in microscopic form, a multi-ethnic community formed around a common language and the one true God. This was the dew drop that was being formed as God began to reveal the working of His Spirit to mankind. The container consisted of Israelites and assimilated Gentiles, and it was NOT a multi-lingual free-for-all culture that was established. It ended up being multi-ethnic, but NOT multi-cultural. There is a difference. And though small, it functioned as one people under one God. From that point forward, this small institution of people became central to the plan of God, and also the target of all evil.

It's important now to remember that because this is the symbol at the beginning of the dispensation, it can be classified as the dew drop, not the deluge. But if this dispensation of time ends like the other two dispensations, with the magnified expression revealed at the end, then at some point in the end of days we will once again see something like this put on display in a people. But in the last days it will be on steroids as compared to the front end. It will be much larger.

Here is what it could look like. In its maturity, in the end of days, the work of the Spirit will produce a nation of Israelites in one geographical place, building their nation as one unified culture centered on Christ. It won't be a mere 120 forming one church under God; it will be a multitude of people joining together to form one nation under God. And they will speak with another language. They will all speak in a new tongue universally understood by the global community around them, and it will be a language that binds the global community together in understanding. And what language might that be? Isaiah says it will be with stammering lips, and from our previous chapter we know how that translates out in a very literal sense. The new tongue will be "gael", and these regathered Israelites will be known as an-gael-ish, or a stammering-lipped people. And lest we forget, many believing gentiles will also be drawn into this same language, culture and expression as well, and these people will be central to the plan of God. They will also be the primary object of hatred by those who are evil.

Remember this; the dew drop at the front of the dispensation does not compare with the deluge at the back end of the dispensation. But in spite of the largeness of what God is putting on display, it will largely be missed by the world and its people. Including the church. Just as in Jesus' day, the religious leaders were too busy with their own agenda to discover God's agenda, and so it will be in this last dispensation of time. God has never intended for the church to merely exist as an institution functioning within a culture. He has intended for the church to become a culture, and there's a big difference between the church functioning as an institution, and the church functioning as a nation. When the church plants a nation in the last days, I submit to you that this is the magnified expression of what God began in this final period of time some 2,000 years ago in _Acts 2_. Could it be that this is what was started at Plymouth Rock some 400 years ago? The House of Israel in one geographical location, speaking a new tongue, joined by the gentile nations around the world. A multi-ethnic nation designed to give glory to God, but certainly not a multi-cultural nation designed to venerate all manner of sin and idolatry.

This is a major story told by many of the prophets in scripture, but the modern church ignores this in favor of living our best lives now. So it will be seen and not understood, primarily because people are looking too small and they tend to get stuck trying to replicate infancy. This story is not told in many churches today because they have a different story of what may happen towards the end. Don't get caught playing institutional church and looking too small! God has ordained that we see and understand the deluge, and when we do we are getting close to the finished work for this era of time. The final show is about to begin.

If we now revisit *1 John 5:7-8* and *2 Peter 3:8*, we can see these baptisms and time equations are physical benchmarks to help us understand His story, better known as history. God has revealed Himself as the Father, Son and Holy Ghost. He has also left physical expressions in these patterns of time, that of water, blood, and the Spirit. An interesting study in and of itself is the transition between dispensations pertaining to the cycle and evolution of government. Before each transition, there is a birth or creation, and the command to establish, rule and govern. Before dispensation #1, there was the creation of Adam and Eve. Before dispensation #2, there was the calling out of Noah. Before dispensation #3, there was the choosing of the disciples. All were birthed and prepared to govern in advance of the time change. Following the actual transition into the new dispensation, they were empowered to establish, rule and govern. Then comes growth & mixture as the wheat and tares grow together. That is a picture of coexistence and friction. But it is not the final picture. The time ends with a birthing of new government in preparation for the upcoming transition, and the new government always survives the upheaval. The transition is when there is a weeding out of the impurities, the pure remains, and a new beginning takes root. If these patterns repeat, we are in for a big shift that will upset the status quo soon. Simply because of the time period that we are moving into on God's calendar. The coming age is not another 2,000 year dispensation; it is the 1,000 year period known as the Kingdom age. And since it has to do with the Kingdom on earth, the battle today is over government! The battle for individual souls has been fought for eons of time. But now is the time when we must battle for the soul of our nation. Now is not the time for the church to take its hands OFF of government! You may have to learn the elements of Kingdom order and government, because we are at the threshold of time in which leaders are chosen and prepared for Kingdom authority after the playing field is leveled. *Ezekiel 38* will level things once and for all in the House of Israel, and you may be called upon to finish the work! That may seem like a tall order, but God believes in your ability to grasp this or He wouldn't have you reading this book. You have come to the Kingdom for such a time as this, now make it count. And while the glory belongs to God, the excitement belongs to us because we are right smack in the middle of the grand finale of all time.

To recap, our timeline looks like this: Until the Millennium, we reside in the age given to human administration. This period stretches from Adam until the end of the present age, or the beginning of the Millennium. That is 6,000 years of cumulative time. Days one through six are given to man, and when we reach the end of year 6,000 on God's clock, life as we know it is done. Why? Day seven is given to the LORD. The seventh 1,000 year day is the Millennium, or the Kingdom age, and it is the final 1,000 year day. It is a day given as a Sabbath rest for the people of God. Evil will finally be put down, and it will be a great time for the righteous here on earth. I'll bet the saints in Heaven can't wait to get back for this! As you study the timeline I laid out at the beginning of this chapter, you can see that man's history is really "His story". Job says it best this way; *Job 5:19 - He shall deliver thee in six troubles* (6,000 years)*: yea, in seven* (the seventh day or the Millennium) *there shall no evil touch thee.* Bring it!

Before I conclude this chapter and move forward into more specifics of great interest, let's review the timeline. According to it, we are getting close to another transition, and there is a lot of associated upheaval with that. For the sake of our study from here forward, we will focus on the end of this present age. There are now almost 6,000 years behind us, and 1,000 years ahead of us, and we are in the time period just preceding Christ's return. This is the transition period that will produce the greatest upheaval the world has ever seen, or will see.

Let's grocery-list a few things that must happen before Christ's return. Prior to the start of the Millennium, all prophecy must be fulfilled. This includes the events of *Ezekiel 38* as detailed in chapter one. The marriage supper of the lamb must take place. There will be wars and rumors of wars. The plagues, vials, and trumpets will be fulfilled. The age of the gentiles must close, and the Jews will turn to Jesus. The Beast system will make its run. And the son of perdition must be revealed. Additionally, the tribulation must take place. Some say it is 7 years; others say it is 3½. For the sake of this study, it matters little at this point. We will look at that later, but it is ancillary to the conversation right now. Regardless of its length, it will happen. And following that Christ must return to establish His Kingdom reign. We have laid out a timeline upon which we can attach the events of scripture. It serves as a backdrop of sorts to help us place the events that we will study.

Before we conclude this chapter, let's revisit a passage that will form our thinking and act as a spring board to launch us forward. We already read it in chapter one, but let's really read it once again.

Ezekiel 39:

> *1 - Therefore, thou son of man, prophesy against Gog, and say, Thus saith the LORD GOD; Behold, I am against thee, O Gog, the chief prince of Meshech and Tubal:*

> *2 - And I will turn thee back, and leave but the sixth part of thee, and will cause thee to come up from the north parts, and will bring thee upon the mountains of Israel:*

> *3 - And I will smite thy bow out of thy left hand, and will cause thine arrows to fall out of thy right hand.*

> *4 - Thou shalt fall upon the mountains of Israel, thou, and all thy bands, and the people that is with thee: I will give thee unto the ravenous birds of every sort, and to the Beasts of the field to be devoured.*

> *5 - Thou shalt fall upon the open field: for I have spoken it, saith the LORD GOD.*

> *6 - And I will send a fire on Magog, and among them that dwell carelessly in the isles: and they shall know that I am the LORD.*

> *7 - So will I make my holy name known in the midst of my people Israel; and I will not let them pollute my holy name any more: and the heathen shall know that I am the LORD, the Holy One in Israel.*

8 - Behold, it is come, and it is done, saith the LORD GOD; this is the day whereof I have spoken.

9 - And they that dwell in the cities of Israel shall go forth, and shall set on fire and burn the weapons, both the shields and the bucklers, the bows and the arrows, and the handstaves, and the spears, and they shall burn them with fire seven years:

10 - So that they shall take no wood out of the field, neither cut down any out of the forests; for they shall burn the weapons with fire: and they shall spoil those that spoiled them, and rob those that robbed them, saith the LORD GOD.

11 - And it shall come to pass in that day, that I will give unto Gog a place there of graves in Israel, the valley of the passengers on the east of the sea: and it shall stop the noses of the passengers: and there shall they bury Gog and all his multitude: and they shall call it The valley of Hamongog.

12 - And seven months shall the house of Israel be burying of them, that they may cleanse the land.

13 - Yea, all the people of the land shall bury them; and it shall be to them a renown the day that I shall be glorified, saith the LORD GOD.

14 - And they shall sever out men of continual employment, passing through the land to bury with the passengers those that remain upon the face of the earth, to cleanse it: after the end of seven months shall they search.

15 - And the passengers that pass through the land, when any seeth a man's bone, then shall he set up a sign by it, till the buriers have buried it in the valley of Hamongog.

16 - And also the name of the city shall be Hamonah. Thus shall they cleanse the land.

17 - And, thou son of man, thus saith the LORD GOD; Speak unto every feathered fowl, and to every Beast of the field, Assemble yourselves, and come; gather yourselves on every side to my sacrifice that I do sacrifice for you, even a great sacrifice upon the mountains of Israel, that ye may eat flesh, and drink blood.

18 - Ye shall eat the flesh of the mighty, and drink the blood of the princes of the earth, of rams, of lambs, and of goats, of bullocks, all of them fatlings of Bashan.

19 - And ye shall eat fat till ye be full, and drink blood till ye be drunken, of my sacrifice which I have sacrificed for you.

20 - Thus ye shall be filled at my table with horses and chariots, with mighty men, and with all men of war, saith the LORD GOD.

21 - And I will set my glory among the heathen, and all the heathen shall see my judgment that I have executed, and my hand that I have laid upon them.

22 - So the house of Israel shall know that I am the LORD their God from that day and forward.

23 - And the heathen shall know that the house of Israel went into captivity for their iniquity: because they trespassed against me, therefore hid I my face from them, and gave them into the hand of their enemies: so fell they all by the sword.

24 - According to their uncleanness and according to their transgressions have I done unto them, and hid my face from them.

25 - Therefore thus saith the LORD GOD; Now will I bring again the captivity of Jacob, and have mercy upon the whole house of Israel, and will be jealous for my holy name;

26 - After that they have borne their shame, and all their trespasses whereby they have trespassed against me, when they dwelt safely in their land, and none made them afraid.

27 - When I have brought them again from the people, and gathered them out of their enemies' lands, and am sanctified in them in the sight of many nations;

28 - Then shall they know that I am the LORD their God, which caused them to be led into captivity among the heathen: but I have gathered them unto their own land, and have left none of them any more there.

29 - Neither will I hide my face any more from them: for I have poured out my spirit upon the house of Israel, saith the LORD GOD.

Lest you despair as you read this, remember who God is for, and who God is against in this scenario. God clearly intervenes for the House of Israel, and stops the invaders cold in the "mountains of Israel". The Rocky Mountains could very well be the place of deliverance for the United States in the coming days. Since we are looking forward, we don't know for sure, but it will depend first and foremost upon how God has determined this to play out. Where ever He draws the line in the sand, and says "enough is enough", the people must have the fortitude necessary to stand their ground. Now is not the time to run; now is the time to stand! God will intervene for His sake, because He is keeping His covenant with the House of Israel. We ARE one nation under God, and there won't be any doubts of that after this event. For the House of Israel, the lights are going to come on! We shall once again know who our national God is, and we will no longer have an appetite for globalism. Additionally, the world community will know this was an act of judgment due to our sin. But it will be turned to our good as God uses it to deliver us from the global chains that seek to bind us. There is a silver lining for those who survive, and it is the restoration that follows; restoration that is, for the House of Israel. We have not yet looked at what is taking place in the world or the House of Judah during this time, or what the Beast system is up to. But believe me, we will. For now, let's challenge a few common assumptions largely adhered to today.

Assumption 1: The church will be gone when this happens. The rapture will occur, and we zing out of here, leaving our clothes neatly folded on the floor.

In response to that assumption, consider this verse:

Ezekiel 39:9 - And they that dwell in the cities of Israel shall go forth, and shall set on fire and burn the weapons, both the shields and the bucklers, the bows and the arrows, and the handstaves, and the spears, and they shall burn them with fire seven years:

If you believe in the rapture as taking place 7 years before the end of time, you are still going to be around for this event. Just do the math. There are 7 years of time after this thing is over, so it's advisable that you prepare to weather the storm. God's pattern has always been to protect His people IN the problem, not remove them FROM the problem. Noah was protected in the flood. Daniel was protected in the lion's den. The three Hebrew children were protected in the fire. God glorifies Himself when you go THROUGH some things victoriously, not when you AVOID things cowardly.

Associated with this train of thought is another verse:

Ezekiel 39:29 - Neither will I hide my face any more from them: for I have poured out my spirit upon the house of Israel, saith the LORD GOD.

This scripture shows the aftermath to be a major time of renewal for the House of Israel! The Spirit of God is still here, and there is a huge revival in our land. Everything is set aright, and this is the time you want to be here! THIS IS WHAT YOU ARE WORKING FOR!!!!!!!! Shall I say it any louder? If God is pouring out His Spirit, and there is a major renewal, America will be largely converted to Christianity during this time. So the Christians are not gone. They have been enabled to take over and finish things up the right way. I want to be here for that.

Assumption 2: The antichrist will rule the entire world at the very end.

First and foremost, there is no "the antichrist" as an individual mentioned in scripture. There is the Beast system and the system and spirit of antichrist, but no "the antichrist" as an individual. The Beast even has some standout leaders in the false prophet and such, but there is no "the antichrist". There is, however, an individual called the "son of perdition", but he is not resident within the Beast system. He has infiltrated the Temple of God, and that is what he calls home. He is working to subvert the people of God as an insider, but he is exposed for who he is before it all wraps up. The Temple belongs to God, and that is what the son of perdition wants. The chapters ahead will bring greater clarity to this matter. Believe me; you do not want to stop reading now.

It begs an interesting question though: Will America be under the control of the Beast system? To answer that question, consider this verse.

Ezekiel 39:7 - So will I make my holy name known in the midst of my people Israel; and I will not let them pollute my holy name any more: and the heathen shall know that I am the LORD, the Holy One in Israel.

Once *Ezekiel 38* is over, The House of Israel (America) will NEVER yield its national sovereignty and culture to a sinful global regime ever again. When God says never, He means never! The Holy One will be IN Israel, so we can't be governed by evil from that day forward. Whatever talons the global system had in the House of Israel have been removed, and we are now free to be one nation under one God. If America goes through this event, only to yield to the system of antichrist, we would be polluting the name of Christ. It leads me to believe that we will be shielded in some way, once we get through the initial assault of Gog and Magog. This is the final affliction for the House of Israel, and while evil may prevail around the world, it has made its final bid to overthrow America. And it fails.

If you are skeptical of my hypothesis, rest assured that I intend to put skin on it in the coming chapters. If I am correct, this will be confirmed in other prophetic scriptures. Scripture must interpret scripture and any position that I espouse. If I am wrong, I don't want to believe the hypothesis, and neither do you. I don't want to sell books full of lies, I want the truth. The authority is the scripture, and we will examine more to come. So we don't have hard evidence to this end yet, but I can lay out a hypothesis based on what we have read so far. It goes something like this: With American military prowess diminished through this war, and Gog destroyed, there will be a vacuum of power. There will be no more restraints against evil. It's a perfect setup for any system of evil to make a final advance around the world. In every place, that is, except the House of Israel. We are going to test that hypothesis with other scripture to prove it RIGHT . . . or prove it WRONG.

In front of us now is a very compelling study. How can we identify the Beast system of the last days? How will it seek to make its final play? How will it affect the global community and the USA? What is the future relationship between the House of Israel (America) and the House of Judah (the Jewish State of Israel)? Who is the son of perdition?

We are just warming up, so proceed at your own risk.

CHAPTER 3

The Beast

If what we've covered so far is new ground for you, admittedly it can be some pretty hard plowing. This is not your typical Sunday morning feel-good message that is presented in a neat little 30-minute window. If you're wrestling with the concepts presented so far, re-read the previous chapters to embed these things into your DNA.

I ended chapter two with a hypothesis that needs to be put to the test. It goes something like this: The House of Israel (America) will be attacked by an alliance of nations, miraculously spared by God, and divinely protected from that point forward. If that hypothesis is going to hold water, it must be reinforced throughout scripture because in the mouth of two or three witnesses everything is established. Until we substantiate it with other scripture, we cannot hang our hat on it, and it needs to be tested. This is what I intend to do, and part of the process will involve a new adventure into *Revelation 13* where we encounter the rise of the Beast system. All of the puzzle pieces will come together at the right time, and everything will intertwine. Until then, let's open up a new front. Here are the writings of John as he saw into the future, with a few comments of my own inserted for clarification:

Revelation 13:

> *1 - And I stood upon the sand of the sea, and saw a Beast rise up out of the sea, having seven heads and ten horns, and upon his horns ten crowns, and upon his heads the name of blasphemy.*

> *2 - And the Beast which I saw was like unto a leopard, and his feet were as the feet of a bear, and his mouth as the mouth of a lion: and the dragon gave him his power, and his seat, and great authority.*

> *3 - And I saw one of his heads as it were wounded to death; and his deadly wound was healed: and all the world wondered after the Beast.*

> *4 - And they worshipped the dragon which gave power unto the Beast: and they worshipped the Beast, saying, Who is like unto the Beast? who is able to make war with him?*

This is the rise of the Beast system. It is shown to be a military power of some kind. So much so, that it appears too strong for anyone to withstand. It is a formidable alliance of nations joined together to oppress and control everything it can.

> *5 - And there was given unto him a mouth speaking great things and blasphemies; and power was given unto him to continue forty and two months.*

The commission of the Beast's run is for a 3½ year period. This is what 42 months equates to. But prior to the Beast's empowerment, the political alliances will form, and there will be time for some precursor events to occur. There will be enough time for one of its heads to be wounded unto death and then healed, and still more time for all of the heads to coalesce. And it will be seen by the world community.

> *6 - And he opened his mouth in blasphemy against God, to blaspheme his name, and his tabernacle, and them that dwell in heaven.*

"Heaven" appears to be the only safe place to be. And the Beast does NOT like the people living there. So much so that he rails against them in what the Bible describes as blasphemy. I wonder why he would occupy his time with people in heaven if his interest is earthly domination. Stay tuned, but for now let's move on.

7 - And it was given unto him to make war with the saints, and to overcome them: and power was given him over all kindreds, and tongues, and nations.

8 - And all that dwell upon the earth shall worship him, whose names are not written in the book of life of the Lamb slain from the foundation of the world.

9 - If any man have an ear, let him hear.

10 - He that leadeth into captivity shall go into captivity: he that killeth with the sword must be killed with the sword. Here is the patience and the faith of the saints.

This Beast system, a system which has raped, pillaged and burned its way across the globe, will come to a just end. The saints are encouraged to be patient and wait for its time to run out.

11 - And I beheld another Beast coming up out of the earth; and he had two horns like a lamb, and he spake as a dragon.

12 - And he exerciseth all the power of the first Beast before him, and causeth the earth and them which dwell therein to worship the first Beast, whose deadly wound was healed.

13 - And he doeth great wonders, so that he maketh fire come down from heaven on the earth in the sight of men,

14 - And deceiveth them that dwell on the earth by the means of those miracles which he had power to do in the sight of the Beast; saying to them that dwell on the earth, that they should make an image to the Beast, which had the wound by a sword, and did live.

15 - And he had power to give life unto the image of the Beast, that the image of the Beast should both speak, and cause that as many as would not worship the image of the Beast should be killed.

16 - And he causeth all, both small and great, rich and poor, free and bond, to receive a mark in their right hand, or in their foreheads:

17 - And that no man might buy or sell, save he that had the mark, or the name of the Beast, or the number of his name.

Here we see the economic reach of the Beast system. It is apparent that everyone alive, with the exception of those who are dwelling in heaven, is subjected to the Beast's oppression through economic control.

18 - Here is wisdom. Let him that hath understanding count the number of the Beast: for it is the number of a man; and his number is Six hundred threescore and six.

This passage focuses on the influence of the Beast system and how it will affect the various people groups of the earth. If you want to pin it to the timeline found in chapter two of this study, these events largely occur in the final 3½ years of the present age which culminates with the return of Christ to usher in the Kingdom age. The only piece that would occur before the final 3½ years is the period where the Beast is wounded and recovers. Refer to the timeline laid out in chapter two and mentally position it on the time continuum accordingly. For the sake of future discussions it is important to solidify when this is happening.

We can't possibly understand everything about this prophecy now, but there are some basics we can resolve. First, these are all symbolic references used to describe events that are occurring on earth. The Beast mentioned in here is not a literal Beast. It is not Godzilla coming up out of the sea to attack Tokyo. No, it is a symbol chosen by God to portray a Beast-like system on earth with human administration. It has heads representative of nations and leaders, and in similar fashion the horns are not literal either. These are symbols of its war machine. In short, everything in this passage is detailed in symbolic form, and we want to put skin on it so we can understand it. That will help us normalize the picture of what John was seeing.

The symbolism points to several tangible things which I have listed below:

- It is a group of united nations, joined together with one thing in mind; to control and oppress.
- Its hatred centers on cultures and people groups associated with Christ, who it then seeks to control and oppress.
- It has an economic system with a long reach, which it uses to control and oppress. This is not a free market system, and you cannot buy or sell without its "mark".
- It has a legal system which creates its laws of governance, and these laws are carried out with the express purpose to control and oppress. Rest assured, there are no checks and balances in this system.
- It has a military / police force for the enforcement of those laws. Which, by the way, is used to control and oppress.

In short, this is a UN system that hates anything in covenant with the God of the Bible.

If we were to read this passage of scripture alone (which is what most Christians do), the immediate assumption is that all of humanity is under its thumb; including the House of Israel. But how do we reconcile verse seven of this chapter with the account of restoration, revival, and protection as detailed in *Ezekiel 39*? Look at the contrasting elements that fuel this dilemma:

Revelation 13:7 - And it was given unto him to make war with the saints, and to overcome them: and power was given him over all kindreds, and tongues, and nations.

Based on this alone, things look bad globally. Contrast that however with what is taking place in the House of Israel after God miraculously spares them from a global assault:

Ezekiel 39:7 - So will I make my holy name known in the midst of my people Israel; and I will not let them pollute my holy name any more: and the heathen shall know that I am the LORD, the Holy One in Israel.

Based on this alone, things look good locally within the House of Israel. Are the prophets on the same page? Is Ezekiel telling one story, and John a different one? How do these two passages correlate?

According to John's account in *Revelation 13*, it looks like everyone on earth is under the Beast's oppression, and the only safe place is in "heaven". If you assume that is a literal reference to heaven, this gives credence to a removal or rapture theory. In all honesty, you WANT to be in "heaven" when this is happening. But we have to ask the question; is "heaven", as it is used in this passage, a literal reference or a symbolic reference? After all, everything else in here is a symbol of something happening on the globe. Why would we change our hermeneutic when we arrive at one word? It is inconsistent interpretation to decree everything to be a symbol, only to turn 180 degrees and decree something else in the same context to be literal. In doing so, we skew the outcome and completely miss the meaning of what is being said. We don't have the answer to that question yet, but the answers are found in the Word of God. It is food for thought, and you will understand with perfect clarity further on in our study.

Up next is the battle with the Beast. And we are still working to flesh out a hypothesis, one that may appear to have holes in it. It goes something like this; The House of Israel (America) will be attacked by an alliance of nations, miraculously spared by God, and divinely protected from that point forward.

CHAPTER 4

The Outer Court

Our last chapter found us in _Revelation 13_ where we witness the rise of the Beast system and its influence over the various people groups of the earth. We understand this to be the final 3½ years of the present age, which culminates in the return of Christ to usher in the Kingdom age.

We can't possibly understand everything about this system now, but we outlined some critical elements worth repeating:

- It is a group of united nations, joined together with one thing in mind; to control and oppress.
- Its hatred centers on cultures and people groups associated with Christ, who it then seeks to control and oppress.
- It has an economic system with a long reach, which it uses to control and oppress. This is not a free market system, and you cannot buy or sell without its "_mark_".
- It has a legal system which creates its laws of governance, and these laws are carried out with the express purpose to control and oppress. Rest assured, there are no checks and balances in this system.
- It has a military / police force for the enforcement of those laws, which is used to control and oppress.

Generally speaking, it is a UN system to be shunned by the people of God, which targets everything in covenant with Almighty God.

In this chapter, we begin the battle with the Beast. And we are still working to test our hypothesis which is as follows: The House of Israel (America) will be attacked by an alliance of nations, miraculously spared by God, and divinely protected from that point forward. At this juncture, based on reading some passages in a stand-alone fashion, it does not appear that our stories jive. One story is told in *Ezekiel 38*, and something apparently different is told in *Revelation 13*. We are working to make heads and tails of the prophetic word. This chapter of our study finds us in *Revelation 11*, and once again I will intersperse my comments in the passage as we move through it. Rest assured, we're working to bring all the pieces of the puzzle together, and it won't be long before things begin taking shape.

Revelation 11

> *1 - And there was given me a reed like unto a rod: and the angel stood, saying, Rise, and measure the Temple of God, and the altar, and them that worship therein.*

As seen in *Revelation 13*, the Beast hates those who are dwelling in "heaven". It obviously cannot get to them, and it obviously cannot oppress them. But it certainly hates them. My immediate hunch in reading this verse is that the "heaven" people of *Revelation 13* are the "Temple" people of this verse. They are protected.

> *2 - But the court which is without the Temple leave out, and measure it not; for it is given unto the Gentiles: and the holy city shall they tread under foot forty and two months.*

Here we are introduced to another people group that is NOT protected. They are referred to here as the "Outer Court" people, and they are troubled and trampled underfoot for a 42 month period. We know that equates to 3½ years, and we can conclude that this is the SAME 3½ year period as seen in *Revelation 13*. Based on that conclusion, we can also assume that the Beast is the trouble maker during this time. It hates both the Temple and the Outer Court, but it can only get to one of them.

> *3 - And I will give power unto my two witnesses, and they shall prophesy a thousand two hundred and threescore days, clothed in sackcloth.*

The Hebrew calendar is a time period of 360 days, and 1,260 days equates to . . . you guessed it . . . 3½ years.

4 - These are the two olive trees, and the two candlesticks standing before the God of the earth.

5 - And if any man will hurt them, fire proceedeth out of their mouth, and devoureth their enemies: and if any man will hurt them, he must in this manner be killed.

6 - These have power to shut heaven, that it rain not in the days of their prophecy: and have power over waters to turn them to blood, and to smite the earth with all plagues, as often as they will.

7 - And when they shall have finished their testimony, the Beast that ascendeth out of the bottomless pit shall make war against them, and shall overcome them, and kill them.

This confirms our assumption that the Beast is the trouble maker, which also confirms the time period of these events. This is the same 3½ year period for both *Revelation 13* and *Revelation 11*.

8 - And their dead bodies shall lie in the street of the great city, which spiritually is called Sodom and Egypt, where also our LORD was crucified.

A quick pause here for a question: What is the name of the great city in which our LORD Jesus was crucified? Its name is Jerusalem, and the spiritual state of it at this time is such that God likens it to Sodom and Egypt. Keep this in mind for further discussion after we finish our trip through this passage.

9 - And they of the people and kindreds and tongues and nations shall see their dead bodies three days and an half, and shall not suffer their dead bodies to be put in graves.

10 - And they that dwell upon the earth shall rejoice over them, and make merry, and shall send gifts one to another; because these two prophets tormented them that dwelt on the earth.

11 - And after three days and an half the spirit of life from God entered into them, and they stood upon their feet; and great fear fell upon them which saw them.

12 - And they heard a great voice from heaven saying unto them, Come up hither. And they ascended up to heaven in a cloud; and their enemies beheld them.

13 - And the same hour was there a great earthquake, and the tenth part of the city fell, and in the earthquake were slain of men seven thousand: and the remnant were affrighted, and gave glory to the God of heaven.

This 3½ year period is drawing to a close, and we are told in the next few verses what happens at the end of it.

14 - The second woe is past; and, behold, the third woe cometh quickly.

15 - And the seventh angel sounded; and there were great voices in heaven, saying, The kingdoms of this world are become the kingdoms of our LORD, and of his Christ; and he shall reign for ever and ever.

By the time we get to the fulfillment of this verse, it is finished! It is time for the Kingdom age to begin. Christ has returned, and the earth now belongs to Him. This is additional evidence confirming that this is not just any 3½ year period; it is the final 3½ year period that corresponds as well to *Revelation 13* and the Beast's run at power.

16 - And the four and twenty elders, which sat before God on their seats, fell upon their faces, and worshipped God,

17 - Saying, We give thee thanks, O LORD GOD Almighty, which art, and wast, and art to come; because thou hast taken to thee thy great power, and hast reigned.

But apparently not everyone is happy about that.

> *18 - And the nations were angry, and thy wrath is come, and the time of the dead, that they should be judged, and that thou shouldest give reward unto thy servants the prophets, and to the saints, and them that fear thy name, small and great; and shouldest destroy them which destroy the earth.*

Contrary to the Earth First movement, this is not an endorsement of radical environmentalism. This is stating that the Beast system which was responsible for wrecking everything for the last 3½ years will be destroyed once and for all.

> *19 - And the Temple of God was opened in heaven, and there was seen in his Temple the ark of his testament: and there were lightnings, and voices, and thunderings, and an earthquake, and great hail.*

And finally we see again that the Temple people have been spared through all of this, and God has certainly been dwelling in the midst of them during this time. They have been experiencing a renewal while the rest of the world and the Outer Court have been dealing with the Beast.

This is an amazing story! It's an intensive overview using symbolism of how the Beast is railing against two people groups, and he can only get to one of them. The challenge now is to normalize the symbolism of what we have read so that we can make sense of it all. To do that, let's discuss the standout events that I commented on briefly as we read through it.

Our first consideration is this; this is the same time period as when the Beast is ruling. *Revelation 13* details this final 3½ year period with the focus on the Beast, but *Revelation 11* details the same time period with a different focus. *Revelation 11* covers the final 3½ year period with its focus being on the Outer Court.

We also see two hated people groups in this passage; the Outer Court people, which is the major emphasis of this chapter . . . and the Temple people, which is the minor emphasis of this chapter. And just who is causing all the trouble for them? *Revelation 13* has already shown us that the Beast system is the aggressor and oppressor during this last 3½ years.

Therefore I would deduce that it is the Beast system stirring up all the trouble.

Our next consideration is this; the symbolism provided to John is a pattern unique to both houses of Israel. Bear in mind that John was a Jew, and he understood that the Temple and Outer Court were found in no other people group on earth. They were central only to Israel. In the layout that God provided to Moses in the initial building of the Tabernacle, the Outer Court was a stepping stone, but the Temple was the destination. The key distinction between the two had to do with their handling of the sacrificial lamb. The Outer Court was the place where the sacrifice was introduced and prepared, but the Temple is where the sacrifice was offered and accepted. The Temple is obviously the place you wanted to be. In a prophetic sense, could the LORD be showing us that one people group was responsible for the introduction and preparation of the Messiah, but they never came to embrace His sacrifice? These would be the Outer Court people. On the other hand, there are the Temple people, who embraced the sacrificed Messiah as the center-piece of their culture. This is the picture being portrayed to John. God is using an overlay of the Temple and Outer Court to paint a picture of two people groups.

John also knew Israel's history, and that they were divided into two distinct camps at the time of his revelation. They were divided into the House of Israel and the House of Judah. Could it be that one is the Temple, and one is the Outer Court? My immediate attention is drawn to that theory because it also fits with how both nations have handled our sacrificed Messiah; Jesus Christ. On display could be the hatred of the Beast towards the two distinct people groups of Israel. This is the Beast vs. the House of Israel and the House of Judah during the final conflict.

We don't know (yet) who these titles represent, but notice the contrast between them. One experiences suffering during this period of great tribulation, while the other experiences protection. So apparently, there is one people group that the Beast cannot touch during this time! They are the Temple in *Revelation 11*, but could they be the House of Israel in *Ezekiel 39* once Gog has been used by God to clean out all the corruption? Could *Ezekiel 38* be a precursor to the final run of the Beast? If so, it sure would be nice to have Ezekiel identify the House of Israel as a Temple people in a definitive way. That would confirm any correlation to them in *Revelation 11:1*. What we do know is that the final conflict of the ages appears to be the Beast vs. the Outer Court and the Temple, and the Temple people are protected.

Let's correlate what we can by weighing this against other scriptures that we've explored. Ezekiel foretold of an evil alliance to rise in the last days, and that alliance is found in *Ezekiel 38*. If that is the foundation, then everything in the New Testament must agree with it. Ezekiel shows a union between Communism and Islam, and the headlines bear that out today. It is taking shape.

Both Islam and Communism are oppressive systems, and are joining forces to establish a united front. These systems may not necessarily be anti-God, but they are both anti-Christ. Look no further than the alliance between Russia and Iran for a very current example. Communism alone is responsible for making more Christian martyrs between 1900 and 2000 than in all of human history leading up to that time. Is it any wonder that God would be against Gog? Alongside of them is Islam. Islam is at war (Jihad) with the "infidel", who they deem to be anything Christian or Jewish. Both Communism and Islam have two primary enemies. They are the United States of America and the Jewish State of Israel. Should Communism and Islam unite and take off the gloves, the world would quite literally have a Beast on its hands. In the words of *Revelation 13*, who could make war with it? For this tyrant's utopia to be realized, who do they both want to destroy? America (the House of Israel) and the Jewish state of Israel (the House of Judah). Isn't it interesting that Communism and Islam have two primary enemies, and what we see in the scripture is the rise of a Beast system that also has two enemies. This is no coincidence.

Can you see how Russia, China, and a variety of Islamic nations could easily form an alliance to become a tyrannical beast? An alliance which has already defined its two primary enemies? This would be an alliance that would make war with the saints, and it is now poised to dominate the world during the end of days. It is happening before our very eyes!

If that sounds like a reasonable assessment, let's take a closer look at a major event in the Beast alliance that occurs before its final 3½ year commission.

I'm referring to the wounding and recovery of one of the Beast's heads. This happens before his final run on global power, and if the alliance taking shape between Communism and Islam is the Beast rising, we have to wonder what or who the wounded head really is. It must be something to do with Communism or Islam if our theory is worth its salt, and it must be something that the global community witnesses. If you interpret the head as a symbol of a person, you begin looking for a head of state to be mortally wounded, only to recover miraculously. But if the symbolism of the head is larger than that of an individual, it opens up a different arena in which to look for a wounding and recovery. If the heads are symbols of nations, this becomes an entirely different picture and event than what we would witness in an individual. Since the Beast is a conglomerate of nations, let's consider it from a national perspective rather than an individual perspective. My personal belief is that since these heads have horns (militaries) and crowns (governments), they represent nations, not individuals. What or who is this head that is wounded and recovers?

Consider that under the presidency of Ronald Reagan, a death blow was dealt both to Communism and radical Islam. He handled the Soviet Union in such a way that they tore down the wall and the USSR broke up. He handled Iran in such a way that radical Islam was wounded and forced underground for years. They quickly released the American hostages when he won his first election, and for good reason. He had no intentions of wasting time with diplomacy; he would have hit them with the full force of America's military. In this context, Reagan's handling of both Communism and Islam was a shot to the head of the Beast, and for many years the world enjoyed the effects. But it is reemerging today. It is coming back to life! Could it be that this was the wounding and recovery of the head of the Beast, and it is once again rearing its head for a final assault against its two primary enemies? We don't know for certain, but the importance of rightly defining the head is not just a substantive issue; it is also a timing issue. If the head is an individual, its wound and recovery are still future events, as well as the time leading up to the final 3½ years of the Beast's oppression. But if the head is national in context, the wound could be history, the recovery a present-day event, and the final 3½ years of oppression could be knocking at the door.

Before I move on from this specific theory, consider carefully one verse found in *Ezekiel 38*. In the first three verses of that passage of scripture, God states that He is against Gog (Russia). As a result, God then reveals a sequence of events He will take Gog through to ultimately bring him to his end. It reads as follows:

Ezekiel 38:

> *4 - And I will turn thee back, and put hooks into thy jaws, and I will bring thee forth, and all thine army, horses and horsemen, all of them clothed with all sorts of armour, even a great company with bucklers and shields, all of them handling swords:*

This verse can be broken down into three distinct phases that Russia will go through before their final push for global dominance. The first phase is a turning back, the second phase is a hook being placed in their jaw, and the third phase is when God brings them forth to wage war. The first phase easily corresponds with the wounding of the head as seen by John in *Revelation 13*. The two prophets tell the same story, they just use different descriptions. The wound that John sees is the turning back that Ezekiel sees. The third steps seen by both prophets also correspond. This is the bringing forth that Ezekiel sees, and the recovery of the head that John sees. They are the same story, and on these two points the stories intertwine. But Ezekiel reveals an interim phase between the wound and the recovery that John does not detail. Ezekiel refers to it as a hook in Russia's jaw. Just what could that be? Mortimer Zuckerman of U.S. News & World Report tells us. In his article on January 22, 2006 entitled Moscow's Mad Gamble, he writes of Iran's nuclear ambitions and Russia's support of Iran. He clearly proves that Russia is the enabling force behind Iran, and is acting as a guardian over them. He states that ". . . *Russia has made the threat more real. It sold the nuclear power plant at Bushehr to Iran and contracted to sell even more to bring cash into its nuclear industry. As one American diplomat put it, this business is a 'giant hook in Russia's jaw.'*" What is the hook in Russia's jaw? It is the profitability of an alliance between a nuclear Iran and itself. Gog is therefore compelled to act as the guardian over Persia's endeavors, and if a clear and present danger to Iran arises, Gog, Magog, Persia, and the remaining alliance will take preemptive action. Even if this means they engage in a surprise attack on the House of Israel. I don't wish to belabor a point that is already clear, but as stated above, the importance of rightly defining the head is not just a substantive issue; it is also a timing issue. If the head is national in context, the wound / turning back are now history. The hook in the jaw has been set, and the recovery / bringing forth to war is soon to occur. Gog is almost ready to make its move, and all it needs is an evil thought to come into its mind.

I stated earlier that the challenge for the student is to normalize the symbolism of what we're reading. Too often we take the symbolism, and make it even more dramatic than what it is. We end up looking for physical Temples to be rebuilt, and at some point we look for a guy to ride in on a pig to desecrate it while his head spins off. This makes for entertaining books, but it also tends to dull our senses to what God is putting on display in plain sight. The goal is not to further dramatize the symbolism of prophecy; it is to normalize it so we can understand it! If you don't, the Messiah could walk your streets and you will want to crucify Him because He doesn't match your dramatic notions.

The Beast is rising, and it is driven by a spirit of hatred for America and Israel. As we continue forward in our study, our goal will be to positively identify the Outer Court and the Temple rather than be satisfied with assumptions. To do that, we have to wrestle with definitions, and continue to use the Word of God to interpret itself. Let's do that with a passage we have already read.

Revelation 13:7 - And it was given unto him to make war with the saints, and to overcome them: and power was given him over all kindreds, and tongues, and nations.

First, some definitions: The word "overcome" means to subdue one's influence. It does not mean that you occupy their nation, but it does mean you effectively put down whatever influence they may have been able to exert. The subdued entity may even remain a sovereign nation, but in overcoming them they no longer hold the position that they used to. They have been marginalized. The next word we want to define is "power" as used in this verse. Power means to have mastery over, jurisdiction over, and rulership over. This indicates direct hands-on oppression rather than just marginalization. Consider these words now in light of the scripture above. The beast "overcomes" (marginalizes their influence) the "saints", but he has "power" (rulership) over everyone else. In essence, his assault on the saints is able to marginalize them and isolate their influence, but he is still not able to rule over them. He really wants to rule over the Temple people, but he cannot touch them. So he rails on them and blasphemes these people in "heaven" whom he cannot get to. He also wants to rule over the Outer Court people, but even though he is able to afflict them for a season, he still can't put them under his thumb. They, too, prevail after a season of affliction.

Next, let's examine the Biblical definition of the word "saints". Most people today would define "saints" as Christians in general. But bear in mind we have had almost 2,000 years to redefine that word according to our frame of reference. We modernize it in the same way we do with "uttermost part". We think of it from our frame of reference and end up being miles off the target. John's frame of reference would have been different. He was schooled in the Old Testament, and I'm sure he read the prophets of old. Interestingly, in the Old Testament this same story is told, but it's obviously not written down by John. It's told by Daniel. *Daniel 12* tells this same story of the final 3½ years, and while it is limited in some of the detail John provides, it clearly illuminates who these "saints" are! Would you like to find out?

Let's take a peak first of all at *Daniel 12:7*. This verse defines the time period and also provides another name for the saints. Let's see what it is:

Daniel 12:7 - And I heard the man clothed in linen, which was upon the waters of the river, when he held up his right hand and his left hand unto heaven, and sware by him that liveth for ever that it shall be for a time, times, and an half; and when he shall have accomplished to scatter the power of the holy people, all these things shall be finished.

In this passage, the "saints" of *Revelation 13* are identified by Daniel as the "holy people". Now, you may wonder how I know these scripture passage refer to the same event and the same people. Well, also in this verse is information showing that these people suffer affliction for "a time, times, and an half" of time. This is a unit of measure referring to 3½. A time is singular, and equals 1. Times are plural, and at a minimum must equal 2.

A half of time is just that. It is a half. Adding each unit together amounts to 3½. This is the same 3½ year affliction targeting the people of God that we have read about in *Revelation 11 & 13*, so it must detail the same players. By these two corresponding reference points, we know that this is the same event as seen from Daniel's perspective. So who are the "holy people" as identified by Daniel, and the "saints" as identified by John? The answer is found in *Daniel 12:1*, which reads as follows:

Daniel 12:1 - And at that time shall Michael stand up, the great prince which standeth for the children of thy people: and there shall be a time of trouble, such as never was since there was a nation even to that same time: and at that time thy people shall be delivered, every one that shall be found written in the book.

The specific people group targeted in the final conflict is identified in this verse as Daniel's people. And since Daniel is an Israelite, this tells us that the dual houses of Israel and Judah are the focus of the wrath of the Beast. He wants to utterly destroy any vestige of the Kingdom of Israel! Either house, both houses, it doesn't matter. He hates them both! This lends further credence to our theory that in *Revelation 11* one house is the Outer Court and the other house is the Temple.

Think of it this way:

- The "saints" of *Revelation 13* are defined as . . .
- The "holy people" in *Daniel 12:7*; which are defined as . . .
- The Kingdom of Israel in *Daniel 12:1* . . .
- Which we know are divided into two kingdoms . . .
- The House of Israel (America) and the House of Judah (the Jewish State of Israel) . . .
- Shown as the Outer Court and Temple in *Revelation 11*.

If you are surprised by the divine harmony in the scripture, don't be. It was all inspired by the same God, and He didn't change His tune along the way. He is telling the same story through a multitude of prophets, and scripture is interpreting scripture! But as it relates to the Outer Court and the Temple, what we don't know yet is who is who. So let's return to *Revelation 11:1-3*.

We return to this passage knowing from *Daniel 12* that the hatred of the Beast will be directed against Daniel's people, who are contained in two distinct parts: the House of Israel (America) and the House of Judah (the Jewish State of Israel). Let's begin with the use of the phrase Outer Court since that is the major emphasis of *Revelation 11*. Who is it referring to? Several indicators, specifically verses 2 and 8, show the Outer Court is connected to literal Jerusalem. The Outer Court is not a religious experience; it is relegated to the geography in proximity to literal Jerusalem. In a national sense, we know Jerusalem is territory held by the House of Judah, so our conclusion is that the term Outer Court refers to the House of Judah.

Why would they be the Outer Court? Simply because of how they have handled the sacrifice of the Messiah. They introduced Him and prepared Him before the face of the people, but they never made Him central to their existence. With regard to the ultimate sacrifice, they are on the outside looking in. That will change, but it has not happened yet. *Zechariah 12* reveals that the House of Judah will look on Him whom they have pierced, and the lights will come on through great suffering. They must make a break from Judaism, for it was just a stepping stone. Christianity is the destination, and their nation must be reformed around the sacrifice of the Messiah Jesus Christ. The government is to be upon His shoulders.

As we conclude this chapter in our study, consider this thought. The scripture ties the people of the Outer Court to a defined geographical location. It is a multitude of people in one geographical area. ALL people in this location will suffer since the Outer Court has to do with a physical location or geography. If our hermeneutic remains consistent, the same must hold true regarding the Temple. If the Outer Court is associated with a geographical area, the same must also be said about the Temple. It too must be associated with a defined people group and geographical location, but unlike the House of Judah, the Temple people have centered their national existence on the sacrificed Messiah Jesus Christ. They are indeed a Christian nation. If it is the House of Israel, scripture must interpret scripture, and we intend to see what the Bible says about the Temple in our next chapter of study. And remember, we're still working to flesh out a hypothesis that sounds like this: The House of Israel (America) will be attacked by an alliance of nations, miraculously spared by God, and divinely protected from that point forward. The appearance of a protected people group in the form of the Temple now makes this hypothesis much more plausible, but stay tuned. The doors of the Temple are about to be opened!

CHAPTER 5

The Temple

I trust you are beginning to understand the importance of rightly dividing the Word when it comes to the distinction between the House of Israel ('saac's sons) and the House of Judah (Jews). This division is the key to understanding Bible prophecy. Without that as your reference point, you quickly get lost. I stated earlier that if you are marginally off in Genesis, you will be miles off in Revelation. Many approach Revelation without knowing what happened in Genesis (the beginning) or much of the Old Testament. They see Revelation as a creative book, rather than an interpretive book. The New Testament prophets, however, are not free to create a new story. What they prophesy must be in complete harmony with the Old Testament, so in that sense the best they can do is interpret and expound upon what the prophets before have decreed. Even Jesus Himself was bound by the authority of the prophetic Word that preceded Him. After all, He inspired it! His utterances of the end times as seen in *Matthew 24* must be in complete harmony with the Old Testament prophets. If not, one of the two is a false prophet, and we know that is not the case. This is also why we constantly use scripture to measure scripture in our pursuit of understanding. We must draw from the treasures of both Old Testament and New Testament (*Matthew 13:52*) if we want the complete picture.

Here is a synopsis of what we have covered so far. In chapter one of our study we examined *Ezekiel 38 & 39* and came to understand the distinction between the House of Israel and the House of Judah. In subsequent chapters of this study we have examined the Beast system of *Revelation 13* and its focus on destroying two major people groups in the final conflict. One people group is known as the Outer Court, and they are the major emphasis in *Revelation 11*. The other people group is known as the Temple, and they are the minor emphasis of *Revelation 11*.

The Outer Court experiences suffering during the final period of great tribulation, while the Temple people experience protection during this same time period.

In our most recent chapter we zoomed in on the Outer Court with the understanding that every title used in *Revelation 11* is a symbolic reference to a modern nation or alliance of nations. We asked the question: Who does the Outer Court refer to? As discovered, the verses of *Revelation 11:2* and *Revelation 11:8* indicate that the Outer Court is connected to literal Jerusalem. In a national sense, Jerusalem is territory held by the House of Judah, not by the House of Israel. God promised the land of Palestine to Caleb and his seed in *Numbers 14:24* with these words: *But my servant Caleb, because he had another spirit with him, and hath followed me fully, him will I bring into the land whereinto he went; and his seed shall possess it.* As seen in *Numbers 13:6*, Caleb was of the tribe of Judah, so not even Ephraim has legal claim to Palestine. Ephraim's land-grant would be in the uttermost parts of the earth, but Palestine belongs to Judah and nobody else. The present Palestinian conflict is simply a result of the world living in rebellion to God's decrees. Jerusalem and all of Palestine belongs to Judah! Since the Outer Court is connected to Jerusalem and the outlying regions, we concluded that the term Outer Court refers to the House of Judah which is the geographical area on a map known as the Jewish State of Israel.

It is important to remember that the Outer Court is tied to a defined geographical location. It is a multitude of people in one geographical area, and it is not a belief system or religious experience. It is a location, and even unlearned Christians will be in the Outer Court when it is trampled underfoot. All people in this location will suffer during this time of great tribulation since it has to do with a physical location or geography. We left off our study with this premise; if the Outer Court is associated with a geographical area, the same must hold true for the Temple. It too must be associated with a defined people group and geographical location. In this chapter of study we intend to find out what the Bible says about the Temple, and labor to identify its location. Believe me, based on the context of *Revelation 11:1*, you want to be dwelling in the Temple when the final conflict gets under way as it is the only place of protection. Let's begin the next leg of our journey as we seek the Biblical definition of the Temple.

We begin with a scripture most associated with the New Testament Temple which is found in *1 Corinthians 3*. It reads as follows:

1 Corinthians 3:16 - Know ye not that ye are the Temple of God, and that the Spirit of God dwelleth in you?

For today's Christian, the simple definition of Temple consists of the redeemed individual. That is where the concept begins, and that is where it ends in their mind. Unfortunately, there is a broader definition for the Temple when it is used in prophecy. It must extend to something beyond that of the individual. An example of this correlates to the events contained within the Temple as seen in *2 Thessalonians 2*. There we see the son of perdition usurping the throne in the Temple . . . in rebellion to Constituted law . . . acting as if he is the people's messiah. He is a narcissist-in-chief and is there in defiance to God. That Temple is something on a larger scale than the individual heart, so the conclusion is that the Temple must have a larger interpretation when it comes to its use in prophetic passages. If Temple is only used in an individual application, the son of perdition is going to be found in the heart of the Christian. He will be a little person inside of you that is on some invisible throne, exalting himself to be God. Frankly, that is not what Paul is talking about in *2 Thessalonians 2*, and it's silly to think that the Temple is limited only to a person's soul. If that is the extent of it, the son of perdition is no more than a bad mood coming from within the Christians. Again, this makes no sense, so we have to look for a larger definition of the term Temple when it is used in the prophetic Word of God. As pointed out a few times now, our hermeneutic must remain consistent as we interpret the symbols used to describe these events. If the Outer Court in *Revelation 11* is a conglomerated people in a specific geographical location, the Temple must follow the same pattern.

Note the use of the word "them" in *Revelation 11:1*. This indicates that a plurality of people exists within the Temple, so it must be something larger than that of the redeemed individual. That alone is proof positive that if we leave our interpretation of Temple at the individual level, it does not fit! And just as with the Outer Court, the Temple is not a belief system or a religious experience. It must refer to a people group in a defined geographical location. It cannot even be relegated to a building of a few thousand square feet that is erected in Jerusalem. It must be something that contains a multitude of people that is not tied in proximity to Jerusalem in any way. The same interpretive baseline applies to both titles, and once we realize that and apply it correctly, we should be able to pinpoint it somewhere on a map, just as we did with the Outer Court.

To fully understand this prophetic title of Temple in *Revelation 11*, we must turn to the source in scripture for the wording used in *Revelation 11:1*. Believe it or not, there is an Old Testament passage that is nearly verbatim to the description given of the Temple in *Revelation 11*. Since the Old Testament precedes the New Testament, we can conclude that the Old Testament reference is the baseline for interpretation as we handle *Revelation 11*. The Old Testament passage I'm referring to is found in *Ezekiel 40* where Ezekiel identifies specifically who the Temple people are. Let's take a look:

Ezekiel 40:

> *2 - In the visions of God brought he me into the land of Israel, and set me upon a very high mountain, by which was as the frame of a city on the south.*

> *3 - And he brought me thither, and, behold, there was a man, whose appearance was like the appearance of brass, with a line of flax in his hand, and a measuring reed; and he stood in the gate.*

> *4 - And the man said unto me, Son of man, behold with thine eyes, and hear with thine ears, and set thine heart upon all that I shall shew thee; for to the intent that I might shew them unto thee art thou brought hither: declare all that thou seest to the house of Israel.*

From verse 4 onward, the measuring of the Temple begins, and the results are communicated. They are not communicated to the global Christian community; they are communicated to the House of Israel! Why? Because they are the Temple people. Out of the two houses of Israel, they stepped into an acceptance of the ultimate sacrifice, while their brother nation of Judah has remained on the fringes to be the Outer Court.

Notice the similarities in how the Temple measurements are communicated in *Revelation 11* and *Ezekiel 40*. Ezekiel is told to rise and measure the Temple, which he then begins to do with a measuring reed. John is also told to rise and measure the Temple with a measuring reed. My conviction is that the word usage by Jesus to describe the Temple in *Revelation 11: 1* correlates to *Ezekiel 40* for a reason. This was a deliberate use of a specific Old Testament passage by Jesus Himself to point us to the right baseline for correct interpretation. *Ezekiel 40* is the foundation to help us understand what the *Revelation 11* Temple is. It is the House of Israel!

Bear in mind that *Ezekiel 40* follows the events of *Ezekiel 38 & 39*. The sequence of chapter and verse does not reveal this, but the context does. *Ezekiel 40* is probably taking place during the time of restoration detailed in *Ezekiel 39*. By this point in time, the House of Israel has been attacked, cleansed, and miraculously spared by God. In essence, the Temple has been cleansed and now it is being protected during the final period when the Beast is raging. According to *Revelation 11*, the Beast cannot get at the Temple and it is livid about this. So it attacks its brother, the Outer Court or the House of Judah. Look at some interesting tidbits from Ezekiel related to the Temple. This is God speaking about the national affairs of America, and it reveals why *Ezekiel 38 & 39* occurred and how God responds after the fact.

Ezekiel 43:

> *1 - Afterward he brought me to the gate, even the gate that looketh toward the east:*

> *2 - And, behold, the glory of the God of Israel came from the way of the east: and his voice was like a noise of many waters: and the earth shined with his glory.*

> *5 - So the spirit took me up, and brought me into the inner court; and, behold, the glory of the LORD filled the house.*

First off, we see that the glory of God inundates the House of Israel at this time. This is consistent with God's declaration in *Ezekiel 39:29*. There He says "*Neither will I hide my face any more from them: for I have poured out my spirit upon the house of Israel, saith the LORD GOD.*" It is renewal time for America! It comes from the east gate, and I wonder if this has to do with the East Coast. That is the seat of power for our nation, and it could be speaking of a renewal that takes place in government. I'm only speculating here, and personally this is the day that I long to see. But wait, there's more:

> *6 - And I heard him speaking unto me out of the house; and the man stood by me.*

> *7 - And he said unto me, Son of man, the place of my throne, and the place of the soles of my feet, where I will dwell in the midst of the children of Israel for ever, and my holy name, shall the house of Israel no more defile, neither they, nor their kings, by their whoredom, nor by the carcases of their kings in their high places.*

Here we see a reiteration of what God decrees in *Ezekiel 39:7; So will I make my holy name known in the midst of my people Israel; and I will not let them pollute my holy name any more: and the heathen shall know that I am the LORD, the Holy One in Israel.* This is God speaking to the House of Israel, and He is showing them to be the Temple people. From *Ezekiel 38* onward, they will never fall into the sins of globalism again. And what are these sins of globalism? Read on.

Ezekiel 43:

> *8 - In their setting of their threshold by my thresholds, and their post by my posts, and the wall between me and them, they have even defiled my holy name by their abominations that they have committed: wherefore I have consumed them in mine anger.*

Apparently, one of God's controversies with the House of Israel was in how they built their nation. They erected a wall of separation between God and their national affairs, and God does not want it there. The progressive arguments of separation of church and state are going to be removed, and the people are instructed to once again allow the laws of God back into public policy. This does not eliminate the checks and balances, or the branches of government, but it does give free reign for Christians to handle the affairs of state. From what I see in scripture, God expects them to! When all of this shakes out, the wall of separation is coming down, and God will step back into our public life because we want Him there.

Ezekiel 43:

> *11 - And if they be ashamed of all that they have done, shew them the form of the house, and the fashion thereof, and the goings out thereof, and the comings in thereof, and all the forms thereof, and all the ordinances thereof, and all the forms thereof, and all the laws thereof: and write it in their sight, that they may keep the whole form thereof, and all the ordinances thereof, and do them.*

> *12 - This is the law of the house; Upon the top of the mountain the whole limit thereof round about shall be most holy. Behold, this is the law of the house.*

Essentially God is telling the House of Israel that they were established to be one nation under one God. And it is going to be a rude awakening that brings shame. God has elevated America above all others because in our founding we were intent on blessing God. We could sing "God Bless America", because as a people we were intent on blessing God. Today however, it's a different story. We have fallen in love with the ways of the global community, and God is going to rip that desire out of our hearts. The "law of the house" for this nation that has been lifted up above all others is that we are to be a holy people. That means we are to be separated to His purposes. This is when the House of Israel will make a crucial discovery. God is not interested in building another church in the nation; He is interested in building the nation into a church. An awakening does not mean that we attend church every day and sing stirring songs; it means that we integrate Christ into every aspect of our national life. The issue God raises with the House of Israel does not center on their church programs. It centers on their failure to integrate His laws into every fabric of their culture. The rude awakening comes when we realize that the church was not designed to be something we do; it is something we are. It was never intended to be an institution functioning within a nation; it was created to become a nation. Only as of late have we settled for the institutionalized model so prevalent today. We are to be a nation of His laws, devoted to His ways, a nation showing forth the praises of the One who has called us out of darkness and into His marvelous light. That will play itself out in every aspect of our society and touch everything. Until that day the church should be a little less self-congratulatory on its polished Sunday productions. Even our immigration policies will be impacted by the laws of God as seen in the next chapter.

Ezekiel 44:

> *6 - And thou shalt say to the rebellious, even to the house of Israel, Thus saith the LORD GOD; O ye house of Israel, let it suffice you of all your abominations,*

> *7 - In that ye have brought into my sanctuary strangers, uncircumcised in heart, and uncircumcised in flesh, to be in my sanctuary, to pollute it, even my house, when ye offer my bread, the fat and the blood, and they have broken my covenant because of all your abominations.*

> *8 - And ye have not kept the charge of mine holy things: but ye have set keepers of my charge in my sanctuary for yourselves.*

> *9 - Thus saith the LORD GOD; No stranger, uncircumcised in heart, nor uncircumcised in flesh, shall enter into my sanctuary, of any stranger that is among the children of Israel.*

Much is said in the Old Testament about immigration and naturalization into Israel's culture. It is a subject in and of itself, but suffice it to say that the LORD gave Israel their immigration policies. It required things of the nation, and things of the immigrant, and it was neither one's prerogative to alter God's policies. Our present behavior of winking at illegal immigration and non-naturalization in the prevailing culture of the House of Israel will cease! Biblical policies are rudimentary to the cultural integrity of we the people, and God will require the House of Israel to face their lax enforcement of His policies head on. To be one nation under God we can be multi-ethnic, but we cannot be multi-cultural. Our culture will once again be centered on the laws of God, and everyone must assimilate upward to that. And for those who do not enter in at the gate, but instead choose to climb over the wall, they will be classified as thieves and robbers and deported.

These are the issues being addressed in the Temple people after they have been cleansed and sealed. They are very practical matters the House of Israel will need to address, and the changes will be sponsored by Almighty God. In a nutshell, God is showing the House of Israel . . . not the House of Judah . . . that they are the Temple. And they have not measured up to His charge. They have allowed . . .

- A wall of separation to exist between their Creator and their national life . . .
- God's name to be polluted through the corrupt moral character of the people . . .
- The money changers to take over through corrupt monetary policies . . .
- Strangers uncircumcised in heart and flesh to come in and pollute due to the lax immigration policies of the nation.

This is just to name a few. These are some of the reasons for the judgment of *Ezekiel 38 & 39*. All of these are SPIRITUAL issues, playing themselves out in our NATIONAL politics. It is a reminder to us that God is just as interested in the affairs of state as He is in the affairs of the church. Once the Temple is cleansed and in a protected state, America must measure up to God's standards and finish the work in righteousness. This is the picture given of the Temple in *Revelation 11*, and it is best understood by reading the details of the same scenario found in *Ezekiel 40* and onward.

Consider the following pattern: Jesus cleansed the Temple building prior to his 3½ year ministry and the same pattern will play out in the last days on a larger scale. When it does, it won't be the cleansing of the Temple building; it will be the cleansing of the Temple people in their Temple nation. When Jesus cleansed the Temple building in His day, He gave us a definition of what the Temple and cleansing would look like, then and now. The first thing He did was cast out the money changers. In like fashion, God is going to collapse the economic system of America to liberate the people. Secondly, he gave us a stark definition of what the Temple will look like. It's found in Jesus' statement; *"My house shall be called a house of prayer for all nations*". This is not just a statement of indignation; it is also a statement of definition that reveals His vision for what the Temple will be. The Temple is ordained by God to be a melting pot of people dedicated to serving God. The way we rightly do that is by being servants of Christ, or Christian in all of our affairs. This is God's design for the Temple.

So in prophetic terms, the Temple must be a conglomerate of people gathered into one place (the geography of the people), adhering to the tenants of Christianity (the spirit of the people). It is a multi-ethnic Christian nation serving Christ, and it is not a stretch to say that Jesus reveals the Temple to be one nation under one God. This is God's intent for the House of Israel, which came to America, and gathered all nations to itself under the banner of being a Christian nation. The Temple is soon to be cleansed.

From our studies we have postulated a sequence of events that will occur at some point in our future. A synopsis looks something like this; *Ezekiel 38 & 39* has yet to occur, and it will happen here in the US. America is the House of Israel, but we are blind to our heritage. We are dwelling in prosperity and safety, and a Communist / Muslim alliance is taking shape that will make its move against us in the near future. America . . . The House of Israel . . . will be dealt a surprise blow. But with the help of God we will prevail! At that point, God will reveal to us that we have been his Temple people, and we have compromised our nation through affinity with the heathen. Right now, America loves everything but God, and we will be cleansed of all our filth. Judgment must begin in the house of God, and only then will we realize that God designed our nation to be a Temple people. However, after God wipes out Gog and Magog, America's diminished power will provide opportunity for the system of the Beast to devour. The vacuum of Christian restraint will create an atmosphere ripe for evil to dominate everything around the globe . . . EXCEPT WITHIN THE TEMPLE! The Temple will not be under any influence of the Beast. Our economic system, education system, justice system, immigration policies, etc. will be free of its grip. Hence, the Beast's hatred for us. Once the Temple is cleansed, she must be divinely protected for the final act. Our commission will be to prepare for a coming family reunion; the marriage between God and the reunified Kingdom of Israel. This is detailed in *Ezekiel 37* and *Hosea 1*; both of which will occur after the Beast system is destroyed and the Outer Court is also cleansed. Rest assured, we will say more of this event in future chapters of study.

We have developed this position on a multitude of scriptures. Getting to this point has required us to slice and dice our way through a maze of timelines, players, scripture passages, and mysteries yet to unfold. It would obviously bring validity to our interpretation of scripture if we had one passage that corroborates this story. Since _Revelation 11_ majors on the Outer Court (the House of Judah), and minors on the Temple (the House of Israel), it would be ideal if we could study a passage that reverses those emphases. We need a passage that tells this same story, but majors on the House of Israel and minors on the House of Judah. This would complete our picture if we could find it. Does such a passage exist? The answer is yes. We will look at it in our next chapter of study.

CHAPTER 6

Lady Liberty vs. The Dragon

Layering scripture is a powerful method to help us understand timing and events. An example is shown in two passages that we have discussed. *Revelation 13* is the final 3½ year period focusing on the Beast. These are events portrayed from the perspective of the Communist and Muslim nations that comprise the Beast. Yet just a few pages back from this is another passage detailing the same period of time, only with a different focal point. *Revelation 11* is the final 3½ year period focusing on the Outer Court. We know this to be the House of Judah. It is interesting to read these as standalone passages, but truly enlightening when we layer them one on top of the other. The big picture comes into view with great clarity when we realize the layers are just different facets of the same stone being shown. The writer chisels at the events from one angle, only to back out and work the issue from a different angle. It is all the same story being told, but as we add more facets to it, that's when it starts to sparkle and we see all the depth and color of the story.

I have previously pointed out that *Revelation 11* has a dual emphasis. The Outer Court (the afflicted people group) is the major emphasis, and the Temple (the protected people group) is the minor emphasis for this final 3½ year period. Our quest now is to find and read one passage of scripture that details the same time period and event, but reverses these emphases. By adding such a passage into the mix, another facet of the story will be seen and our understanding will gain clarity. In this chapter of study we will read a passage of scripture that emphasizes the protected people group, and minors on the afflicted people group. Another layer is about to be added.

Up next is *Revelation 12*. As has been my custom, a few comments will be inserted where deemed important, and a full discussion of this passage will be presented at length subsequent to our reading. For now, engage your mind in the most important piece of the equation . . . the unerring Word of God.

Revelation 12:

> *1 - And there appeared a great wonder in heaven; a woman clothed with the sun, and the moon under her feet, and upon her head a crown of twelve stars:*

> *2 - And she being with child cried, travailing in birth, and pained to be delivered.*

> *3 - And there appeared another wonder in heaven; and behold a great red dragon, having seven heads and ten horns, and seven crowns upon his heads.*

First of all, take note that this dragon has seven heads and ten horns. It is called a dragon here, but its ornamentation reveals that it is the Beast of *Revelation 13*. The seven heads and ten horns are the tell-tale signs to that end, and in this passage it simply has a different label and description. It is called the great red dragon!

> *4 - And his tail drew the third part of the stars of heaven, and did cast them to the earth: and the dragon stood before the woman which was ready to be delivered, for to devour her child as soon as it was born.*

> *5 - And she brought forth a man child, who was to rule all nations with a rod of iron: and her child was caught up unto God, and to his throne.*

> *6 - And the woman fled into the wilderness, where she hath a place prepared of God, that they should feed her there a thousand two hundred and threescore days.*

The time frame of this woman's protection amounts to 1,260 days. Based on the Hebrew calendar-year of 360 days, this amounts to 3½ years. The time period immediately prompts a question; is this the same 3½ year period detailed in *Revelation 11 & 13*? Or is it a different 3½ year period? We are certain to find out, but not quite yet.

> *7 - And there was war in heaven: Michael and his angels fought against the dragon; and the dragon fought and his angels,*

> *8 - And prevailed not; neither was their place found any more in heaven.*

> *9 - And the great dragon was cast out, that old serpent, called the Devil, and Satan, which deceiveth the whole world: he was cast out into the earth, and his angels were cast out with him.*

> *10 - And I heard a loud voice saying in heaven, Now is come salvation, and strength, and the kingdom of our God, and the power of his Christ: for the accuser of our brethren is cast down, which accused them before our God day and night.*

> *11 - And they overcame him by the blood of the Lamb, and by the word of their testimony; and they loved not their lives unto the death.*

> *12 - Therefore rejoice, ye heavens, and ye that dwell in them. Woe to the inhabiters of the earth and of the sea! for the devil is come down unto you, having great wrath, because he knoweth that he hath but a short time.*

> *13 - And when the dragon saw that he was cast unto the earth, he persecuted the woman which brought forth the man child.*

> *14 - And to the woman were given two wings of a great eagle, that she might fly into the wilderness, into her place, where she is nourished for a time, and times, and half a time, from the face of the serpent.*

Just as in *Daniel 12*, this reiterates the length of time for this event as a time, times, and a half of time. I previously pointed out that a time is singular, times are plural, and a half of time is just that; a half. Adding the sum of the "times" equates to 3½. This is the final 3½ year period, and the

Woman is kept in a safe place for that duration. But only after an initial fight with the dragon.

> *15 - And the serpent cast out of his mouth water as a flood after the woman, that he might cause her to be carried away of the flood.*

> *16 - And the earth helped the woman, and the earth opened her mouth, and swallowed up the flood which the dragon cast out of his mouth.*

> *17 - And the dragon was wroth with the woman, and went to make war with the remnant of her seed, which keep the commandments of God, and have the testimony of Jesus Christ.*

This passage is a picture of lady liberty vs. the red dragon. Once again our goal is not to further dramatize the symbolism of prophecy; it is to normalize it so we can understand it! For starters, if we expect to understand what this IS saying, we must first understand what it is NOT saying. I'll begin by addressing two common misperceptions which this CANNOT be referring to:

Misperception #1: This is an account of the House of Judah and the birth of Christ 2,000 years ago.

Fact: This cannot be, and that interpretation does not fit for several reasons;

- After Mary gave birth to the Messiah, the House of Judah did not flee to the wilderness for 3½ years to evade any kind of dragon or beast.
- After Mary gave birth to the Messiah, Jesus was not caught up to God and His Throne as soon as He was born.
- There was no heavenly war at Christ's birth. Rather, the angels demonstrated heavenly joy to the shepherds when they announced the birth of our Savior.
- There was no remnant having the testimony of Jesus that the dragon was able to afflict when it could not devour Mary's child Jesus. Nobody existed at that time with a testimony of Jesus so *Revelation 12:17* was not even possible in that era of time.

- Finally, it does not fit what I call the "90 AD" rule laid out in *Revelation 4:1*.

What is the "90 AD" rule, you ask? Well, it's pretty simple to understand and it is based on the content of *Revelation 4:1*. There we find the Word of the LORD to John as this: *After this I looked, and, behold, a door was opened in heaven: and the first voice which I heard was as it were of a trumpet talking with me; which said, Come up hither, and I will shew thee things which must be hereafter.* In this verse the LORD reveals to John that what he is about to see are things which "must be hereafter". In other words, what John writes about from *Revelation 4:1* to the end of the book are events yet to take place in the future. He is not going to be shown historical events; he is going to be shown future events. And since it is estimated that John received this vision on the isle of Patmos in the year 90 AD, the birth of Christ was already close to a century in the past. It was a historical event, not a future event. So the fulfillment of *Revelation 12* must be in the future at some point beyond the year 90 AD. If you want to know exactly when the event will be fulfilled, look no further than the content and the time period of the details for the necessary clues. This is the same period of time as *Revelation 11*, *Revelation 13*, and *Daniel 12*. It is during the last 3½ years. It is not just ANY 3½ year period; it is the FINAL 3½ year period when this will be fulfilled. It cannot be referring to the House of Judah giving birth to the Messiah.

Misperception #2: This is a picture of a spiritual battle in literal heaven, regardless of its timing.

Fact: As used in this passage, this is not literal Heaven existing beyond the realm of human sight. "Heaven" as it is used in *Revelation 12* is defined as:

- A place where the enemy has gained a foothold. This certainly does not describe the heaven that exists in another dimension.
- A place where satan can intimidate, persecute, and devour. Satan is IN this Heaven as it is used in this passage, and he is working to afflict the people there. Literal heaven is not a place where satan has access or influence.
- A place of a great last day war that opens the stage to the final 3½ year conflict. Literal heaven is not a place of war.

- A place you have to leave in order to go to God. The Manchild leaves this Heaven to go to God and to His throne. Apparently, this is not the heaven where those things are.
- A place where mortality exists. Death is even possible here. The victory requires that people love not their lives unto the death. This does not describe a spiritual battle; this describes a physical battle in which people actually die.

Can you see how easy it is for error to creep in when we mix interpretive attributes to the symbolism used? There is often a mixed grid used to filter the symbolism, and it usually looks something like this:

- The Dragon—he is a symbolic entity.
- The Woman—she is a symbolic entity.
- The Stars—they are symbolic entities.

Then comes the shift in our interpretive baseline:

- The Manchild—he is a literal child.
- The Birth—it is a literal birth.
- Heaven—it is literal and exists in an unseen dimension.

By changing our hermeneutic in mid-stream, the outcome is a skewed interpretation that leaves us blind to the revelation. It leads us to one dangerous conclusion:

- The war—it is spiritual and takes place in an unseen realm.

Nothing could be further from the truth.

In reality, Heaven as it is used in _Revelation 12_ is a symbolic name. We don't know what it is yet, but apparently it is central to the plan of God on earth, and the primary object of the Beast's wrath. It is the same Heaven the Beast is railing against in _Revelation 13:6_. It is where the Woman dwells, and also a place that Satan has access to for a time until he and his minions are thrown out. He has infiltrated it because he wants this Heaven to be his own. To understand the passage, we must interpret this Heaven with the intent of driving this passage's fulfillment to earth where it belongs.

This entire story contained in _Revelation 12_ will play out somewhere on planet earth. And now that we know what _Revelation 12_ is NOT speaking of, the obvious question remains; what IS it speaking of?

Our first clue is given to us in the time period. The bulk of _Revelation 12_ is the SAME time period as _Revelation 11 & 13_, but it also includes the lead up elements that precipitate the run of the Beast/Dragon for the final 3½ years. Unlike _Revelation 11_ however, the major emphasis in _Revelation 12_ is on the protected people group; known here as the "Woman" in the "Wilderness". The minor emphasis is on the afflicted people group, seen in the last verse as a "Remnant" which is related to the Woman. This is the same picture as _Revelation 11_, but with a reverse emphasis on the players, and different labels used to describe them. Furthermore, if this is the same event as _Revelation 11_, we also know it is the same event that Daniel details in _Daniel 12_. It is:

- The same event (the final conflict) . . .
- The same location (earth) . . .
- The same time period (the final 3½ years) . . .
- The same national players (The Beast vs. the House of Israel and the House of Judah) . . .
- A different emphasis (focusing here on the House of Israel) . . .
- With different labels (Woman instead of Temple, Remnant instead of Outer Court, Dragon instead of Beast).

Let's solidify this train of thought so can proceed. Things get really interesting from this point forward, and a firm grasp on what I have presented to this point is necessary. Based on what we know from _Revelation 11_, there is only one entity that is protected during the final conflict. There it is called the Temple, which we know according to _Ezekiel 40-48_ is the House of Israel (America) after her cleansing. In _Revelation 12_ she has a new label; a Woman in the Wilderness, after the onslaught of the Dragon. The actual assault of the Dragon against her is a small window of time that precedes his final 3½ year tear around the globe, but when he realizes the Woman is protected and he can't get at her, he turns his wrath against a Remnant that is related to her. The Woman remains protected for the final 3½ years. The story looks like this:

- The Temple of *Revelation 11* . . .
- Is the Woman of *Revelation 12* . . .
- Understood by *Ezekiel 40-48* to be the House of Israel . . .
- After the onslaught of Russia/China/Iran in *Ezekiel 38* . . .
- Shown from John's perspective in *Revelation 12* as the initial attack by the Dragon.

Read those bullet items through slowly and make sure you really understand how they interconnect. Christ too, is showing us today some things which must be hereafter. Our conclusion thus far: In *Revelation 12*, Heaven is the symbolic reference given to the House of Israel's home . . . on earth . . . in the last days. If you harbor any doubts, read on.

Listen to how Jesus defines Heaven in the last days, in His own words:

Matthew 13:

> *24 - Another parable put he forth unto them, saying, The kingdom of heaven is likened unto a man which sowed good seed in his field:*

> *25 - But while men slept, his enemy came and sowed tares among the wheat, and went his way.*

In Jesus' rendition of heaven, men are the guardians of it. Men have the watch over the heaven He is describing here. And because men have not been vigilant over heaven, the enemy has gained a foothold in it.

> *26 - But when the blade was sprung up, and brought forth fruit, then appeared the tares also.*

> *27 - So the servants of the householder came and said unto him, Sir, didst not thou sow good seed in thy field? from whence then hath it tares?*

A state of coexistence now exists in this heaven. Evil is apparently able to live and grow here for a season. How long we do not know yet, but the answer is soon to come.

28 - He said unto them, An enemy hath done this. The servants said unto him, Wilt thou then that we go and gather them up?

An enemy in heaven? The results of which are showing up in heaven? This is preposterous! Unless of course, this heaven is a symbol of something taking place on earth. Read on to see how this problem is resolved.

29 - But he said, Nay; lest while ye gather up the tares, ye root up also the wheat with them.

30 - Let both grow together until the harvest: and in the time of harvest I will say to the reapers, Gather ye together first the tares, and bind them in bundles to burn them: but gather the wheat into my barn.

The time of separation comes at the very end. Evil is removed from this heaven, the righteous remain and are protected in what He describes as His barn. So the woman has her wilderness, and the wheat has its barn. Both are in heaven. Are they one in the same? Is this the literal heaven that Jesus is describing in the parable? Like you and I, the disciples want a straight-up rendition of last-day heaven to clear these questions up. Jesus does not disappoint:

36 - Then Jesus sent the multitude away, and went into the house: and his disciples came unto him, saying, Declare unto us the parable of the tares of the field.

37 - He answered and said unto them, He that soweth the good seed is the Son of man;

38 - The field is the world; the good seed are the children of the kingdom; but the tares are the children of the wicked one;

In the parable, Heaven is the field, and Jesus plainly decrees that this Heaven is on earth. Additionally, He describes rightful citizens as the children of the kingdom. The only kingdom known to the disciples was the kingdom of Israel, so their immediate assumption would be that the children of the kingdom were Israelites, and Jesus is calling their home Heaven.

39 - The enemy that sowed them is the devil; the harvest is the end of the world; and the reapers are the angels.

Once again, it is seen that in this Heaven, the devil has access. Just as in *Revelation 12*.

40 - As therefore the tares are gathered and burned in the fire; so shall it be in the end of this world.

The separation of the good and evil out of this heaven is reserved for the very end of days, also consistent with *Revelation 12*.

41 - The Son of man shall send forth his angels, and they shall gather out of his kingdom all things that offend, and them which do iniquity;

42 - And shall cast them into a furnace of fire: there shall be wailing and gnashing of teeth.

The dragon is thrown out, and he is upset!

43 - Then shall the righteous shine forth as the sun in the kingdom of their Father. Who hath ears to hear, let him hear.

And lastly, even though the tares are upset to the point of weeping and gnashing their teeth, the righteous remain in this heaven in a protected state, and they are now free of the coexistence they had endured for so long.

The similarities between this and *Revelation 12* are plain to see to anyone with an objective mind. In both passages we see a place where the enemy coexists with Israel, and a violent separation between the two takes place in the last days. They sound like the same event and same place! Frankly, that makes sense because Jesus is the one telling the story to both writers. In one instance He tells all the disciples, and Matthew captures the details. Some 60 years later He tells the same story to John on the isle of Patmos, and he captures it in Revelation. Why change the story, when it is THE story?

Too often we are guilty of hearing what we want to hear as we read the Word. Jesus CLEARLY tells us that the Kingdom of Heaven is an earthly entity. He never refers to it as the Kingdom IN Heaven, yet that's usually what we often hear. It is described as the Kingdom OF Heaven; and that is a statement of origin, not a statement of location. It's like a "Made in China" sticker showing where something is from, not where it is located. The next time you are in your kitchen, grab a pot and look on the bottom of it. It will likely say "Made in China", and it will help you to remember that a stamp of origin is not a declaration of its location. The pot is in your kitchen, though it did not originate there. The Kingdom of Heaven is on earth, though it did not originate with earthly thinking. It is not man's idea; it is God's. I submit to the reader that based on the similarities in these two passages, it is entirely likely that this heaven in _Matthew 13_ is the same heaven of _Revelation 12_. Once again we find complete harmony in the Word of God, and this should come as no surprise.

As we consider the proper use and definition of Heaven in these passages, consider the following. F.L. Hoffman in his book "Thy Kingdom Come" states that the word "America" means "The Kingdom of Heaven". How does he come to this conclusion? The word "America" is derived from the old Norse word "Ommerike". "Omme" means "ultimate" or "final" and "Rike" means "kingdom". "Ommerike" would translate as "the ultimate kingdom". From there he points out that "Ommerike" is a slightly corrupted form of the more ancient Gothic word "amalric". "Amal" means "heaven" and "ric" means "kingdom". Going further, he illustrates that the Gothic word of "Ammaric" is the German word "Himmelreich", which is used in the German New Testament to mean "Kingdom of Heaven". Thus, "Amalric", "Himmelreich", "Ommerike" and "Ammarica" are synonymous terms for the "Kingdom of Heaven". C.R. Dickey in his book "One Man's Destiny" refers to Heaven in this fashion; _"Heaven as used in Revelation, has a definite relationship to the condition existing ON EARTH within the House of Israel in the last days"_.

To that I must agree! In contrast to tyrannical governments existent throughout the world, the regathered House of Israel in "Ammarica" is truly heaven on earth. This explains the reason why everyone wants to . . . A) be a part of her, or . . . B) destroy her. I don't know about you, but as for me, I pledge allegiance to flag of the United States of The Kingdom of

Heaven (Ammarica)! And to the Republic for which it stands, one nation under one God, indivisible, with liberty and justice for all!

Listen to how key verses in *Revelation 12* sound when we substitute the word "heaven" with the Gothic word "Ammarica".

Revelation 12:

> *1 - And there appeared a great wonder in "Ammarica"; a woman clothed with the sun, and the moon under her feet, and upon her head a crown of twelve stars:*

> *3 - And there appeared another wonder in "Ammarica"; and behold a great red dragon, having seven heads and ten horns, and seven crowns upon his heads.*

> *4 - And his tail drew the third part of the stars of "Ammarica" . . .*

> *7 - And there was war in "Ammarica": Michael and his angels fought against the dragon; and the dragon fought and his angels,*

> *8 - And prevailed not; neither was their place found any more in "Ammarica".*

> *9 - And the great dragon was cast out, that old serpent, called the Devil, and Satan, which deceiveth the whole world: he was cast out into the earth, and his angels were cast out with him.*

> *10 - And I heard a loud voice saying in "Ammarica", Now is come salvation, and strength, and the kingdom of our God, and the power of his Christ: for the accuser of our brethren is cast down, which accused them before our God day and night.*

> *11 - And they overcame him by the blood of the Lamb, and by the word of their testimony; and they loved not their lives unto the death.*

> *12 - Therefore rejoice, "Ammarica", and ye that dwell (there). Woe to the inhabiters of the earth and of the sea! for the devil is come down*

unto you, having great wrath, because he knoweth that he hath but a short time.

Fascinating!

Let's take a closer look at the Woman knowing that she is symbolic of the House of Israel. What we want to examine are her characteristics to see if they appear in our nation today. After all, if America is the Woman, and we live in the last days, the description of her should fit our nation perfectly.

First, there are 12 stars upon her head. These are symbols of all 12 colonies of Israel. Behold how good and how pleasant it is when brethren dwell together in unity! The Woman is the melting pot for all the colonies of Israel, and this fits who we are as a people.

Next, she has her feet on the moon. This represents the foundation upon which she stands as a people, and throughout scripture the moon is representative of Jesus. No man can see the face of God and live, just as no man can look upon the sun and retain his eyesight. Jesus however was the reflected light of the Father, just as the moon is the reflected light of the sun. In the last days the moon is turned to blood, a symbol of Jesus shedding His blood. The moon is unimaginably cratered above all other heavenly bodies, representing the broken body of Jesus. This Woman is a nation built upon the rock of Jesus Christ! So it's fitting for God to provide confirming evidence of these facts in the physical realm. America is the only nation to place men on the moon. The exact count is twelve men. That is one for each of the tribes of Israel. The only nation to place its feet on the moon is the House of Israel, the Woman! This was allowed by God to show us loud and clear who we are and what our foundation is as a nation!

Lastly we see she's a woman with a crown. America's national symbol is the statue of liberty, and she is wearing a crown. She is known to the world as Lady Liberty! The red dragon is the national symbol of China, which is Communist and in alliance with Russia. *Revelation 12* is a picture of lady liberty vs. the red dragon! The symbolism could not be any clearer!

The dragon attacks her on her own turf in the last days, only to be kicked out completely so she can be divinely protected! The front end of *Revelation*

12 is *Ezekiel 38* as revealed to John on the isle of Patmos. Gog attacks to overthrow her, even to the point of casting out of his mouth a flood (an invasion). Ultimately he loses his bid to defeat her, and God rules COMPLETELY over His nation for the final 3½ years. But what is an angry dragon to do when it can't defile the Temple / Woman? It goes after the Woman's seed known as the Remnant. This is the House of Judah, also known as the Outer Court in *Revelation 11*. The Remnant is of the woman's seed, so they are related entities. In complete harmony with *Revelation 12:17*, the House of Judah is the one nation that adheres to the commandments of God as given through Moses, and they alone have the testimony of Jesus. The House of Judah is the only nation that can lay claim to the fact that Jesus walked their streets. When all these passages are layered one on top of the other, we have strong evidence that *Revelation 11*, *Revelation 12*, *Revelation 13*, *Daniel 12*, and *Ezekiel 38 & 39* are the same events with different emphases and perspectives. We should not read one without reading the others.

As we prepare to close this chapter of study, there is one critical issue that has not been clarified; it is the "birth" of the Manchild. He and his birth are critical because it tips the hand of the Beast, and forces it to make its move. The Manchild is a mortal threat to the dragon's system, and his birth enrages the dragon. Whatever this birth is will be plainly seen by all, including the dragon and the House of Israel. It is the last cursory event to initiate the final conflict, and we need to know what it is. Who or what could the Manchild be, and what is his birth?

Answers are made easier when we apply our interpretive baseline consistently to both the Woman and the Manchild. If the Woman is a national entity, the Manchild must be a national figure "birthed" by the entire nation. He is something the entire House of Israel is engaged in producing, so he is something national in scope. Additionally, he is a leader. He is not brought forth to be a local leader or state leader; he is a national leader. He is someone brought forth with the intent AND the capability of ruling ALL nations with a rod of iron. We conclude that he must have a large enough platform and office from which to do that. He cannot be a mayor, governor, or senator, because those platforms are too limited to accommodate what his assignment is.

When framed in this light, it becomes easier to see what is not yet in view. The only national offspring capable of functioning with this power and authority is the President of the United States. Whoever occupies that position holds the most powerful office in the world. My hypothesis is this; the Manchild is a symbol of a future President, a leader brought forth by the entire nation. Associated with that, the references to his birth would be symbolic of an election or appointment. This is not an ordinary election; it is one that is very painful and laborious for the nation. It is a birther battle of epic proportions! The Manchild is of the Woman's seed, and probably has a valid birth certificate to prove it. The dragon's choice however would be someone completely different. It would favor an imposter, a fraud. Someone of his seed, with no allegiance to the culture that God has vested in the House of Israel. Someone who will sell out the culture of Christ to her enemies if given the chance. Everything comes to a head in this final battle for the highest office of the land in the United States of America.

I recognize that we have not reached this moment of time yet, and our forward look carries with it a degree of speculation. But by building line upon line, and precept upon precept, our speculation is built on a consistent foundation. It is also built on the principles of normalization that I've stressed several times. The real work of handling the mysteries of scripture is not to further dramatize it, but rather to normalize it. This is what I've set out to do. If this assessment is accurate, the stage is rapidly being set for the final conflict.

On the premise that these conclusions are correct, play the scenario forward and think of what America may soon experience. Something of a national crisis could produce a vacuum of power in the executive office, thus necessitating blood, sweat and tears to produce a legitimate leader. It would have to be some crisis larger than what we have ever experienced, and leave us struggling to establish a chain of command that is Constitutional. The backlash could create a very polarized uprising in both camps, and a strong President-Elect that the dragon hates. The Manchild is not a picture of group hugs and harmony with the global system. He is fed up with progressivism and globalism, and he carries a worldview that is unacceptable to the system which wants to dominate the Woman. The Manchild intends to rule from a position of strength and national sovereignty rather than apologetics and acquiescence. He does not gain his position of leadership by apologizing to the world for America's greatness and strength. He fully intends to use that strength to subdue our national enemies. This is in direct opposition to the philosophy and system favored by the Dragon, which has infiltrated the power structure of the Woman's government. His tail draws "the third part of the stars of heaven", which alludes to more than a generic reference to 33% of the population. It draws THE third part, not just A third of the total. To illustrate, if I were to place blocks of wood shaped as the letters A, B, and C on a table, and tell you that you could have 1/3 of them, you could pick any of the letters. A, B, or C would fulfill the fraction of 1/3. But if I said you must take *the third part*, you are only left with one option, and that is the letter C. It is the third letter, and it is the only one that fulfills the definition of the third part. So what does the third part refer to in *Revelation 12*? Revisiting the scriptural inspiration behind America's branches of government may give us a clue. As stated in the Forward, *Isaiah 33:22* reads *"For the LORD is our judge, the LORD is our lawgiver, the LORD is our king; he will save us."* The recreational reader quickly misses the three branches of government represented in this verse: The Judicial branch (the LORD as judge), the Legislative branch (the LORD as lawgiver), and the Executive branch (the LORD as king). *Isaiah 33:22* is the foundation for our Constitutional balance of powers, and in this context the third part or third branch of government is the Executive branch. In *Revelation 12*, it appears the dragon has taken hold of the Executive branch as his own.

As you will see in our next chapter of study, the Dragon will have its own leader in charge of the third branch of power for a season at the end; and with the birth of her Manchild the Woman is positioned to take it back. This utterly infuriates the Dragon, and this is why the process is so laborious. The Dragon is not interested in a 4-year term, or an 8-year term. Once it has the power, it never intends to relinquish it. The Dragon wants to rule the House of Israel (and the world), and the conflict in *Revelation 12* amounts to a battle for the seat of power over the entire globe. In the last days that power is held by the House of Israel, and the seat of power is found in the Oval Office of the White House. Whoever occupies that office effectively governs the entire world. The Dragon / Beast system realizes that it will lose its grip if the Manchild survives beyond his birth, and it is forced to take extreme measures. The hook is placed in its jaw, and it assassinates the Manchild in his infancy; a President-Elect not yet inaugurated. In military terms it is called a decapitation strike. When an enemy smites the shepherd, the sheep scatter. Especially when the people are fat and lazy mentally. It also creates an opportune moment to escalate the attack and launch a full-scale invasion as seen in the Dragon casting out of its mouth a flood. A decapitation strike against a slumbering people, during a transition of power, chaos, and infancy of a new leader would create a perfect environment for the enemy to make its move. Normally speaking, the time between an election and an inauguration is moving into the winter months, which would maximize the suffering and demoralization of the people forced to flee inland away from the invaders. This would create the winter flight followed by great tribulation that Jesus refers to in _Matthew 24_. Everything fits like a hand in a glove.

While _Revelation 12_ provides details surrounding the birth of the Manchild . . . in Heaven or the Temple . . . there is another event likely taking place at the same time and in the same place. It is not detailed in _Revelation 12_, but it is found in another passage of scripture we have yet to study. It is likely THE event that precipitates this birth, and the reason it is filled with blood, sweat and tears for the House of Israel. We intend to explore this in our next chapter of study. The son of perdition is about to be revealed in the Temple.

CHAPTER 7

Treason in the Oval Office

What could possibly produce a Constitutional crisis and vacuum of leadership large enough to create havoc in Heaven as the Woman labors to produce a leader? I'm referring of course to the events described in _Revelation 12_. Obviously this is no ordinary birth, and it is uncharted waters for the Woman. It is also a scenario which has the Dragon fuming. As pointed out a few pages back, if "the third part of the stars of heaven" is the Executive branch of government, the Dragon has no intention of relinquishing its grip on power. Add to this many "'saac's sons" who have defected to the side of evil, or fallen away, and you have the makings of a civil war. There is no middle ground. You are either for the Woman, or you are for the Dragon, and a fight over this birth is inevitable.

The answer may be found in yet another passage of scripture dealing with the events of the Temple, which we know according to _Revelation 11:1_ and _Ezekiel 40-48_ is the House of Israel or America. Another facet is about to be chiseled into the body of knowledge we have already acquired. Our opening text for this chapter of study is found in _2 Thessalonians 2_. Consider its words.

2 Thessalonians 2:3-4:

> _3 - Let no man deceive you by any means: for that day shall not come, except there come a falling away first, and that man of sin be revealed, the son of perdition;_

> _4 - Who opposeth and exalteth himself above all that is called God, or that is worshipped; so that he as God sitteth in the temple of God, shewing himself that he is God._

Prior to the end of all things, a falling away will occur within the Temple. This speaks of a defecting from the truth. Additionally, the "man of sin" is revealed in the Temple. The man of sin is titled the "son of perdition", and he has usurped the throne in the TEMPLE. He is described as a narcissist-in-chief, even to the extent of believing that he is the people's messiah. He believes that HE is the change the people need, which is certainly a tall order for a mere mortal. For him to truly believe his own lies he must be one deceived individual. Sadly many of the Temple people are equally deceived because many side with him. They have defected from the truth to support the wrong side. The important thing to note is that while the son of perdition is certain to embody the values of the Beast system, he is not found within the Beast. He is found IN THE TEMPLE, and this is why I've spent considerable time in previous chapters wrestling with the right definitions of Temple, Heaven, and so forth. Definitions matter! If we do not rightly divide the Word of Truth, we end up studying it the wrong way. There must be a wrong way to divide the Word for Paul to warn Timothy to study and divide the scripture the right way (*2 Timothy 2:15*). As it applies to our study, right definitions of the terms and labels will help us pinpoint where these events will take place. Incorrect definitions can place us miles off the target and blind us to events taking place right in front of us. The location for the usurpation of the son of perdition is in a very specific location. It is in the Temple, and as you will see in a moment the power that he holds over the people appears to be illegitimate. In light of these things, the Apostle Paul then encourages the reader to understand and take heart because the son of perdition will be revealed for who he is and cast down.

> *7 - For the mystery of iniquity doth already work: only he who now letteth will let, until he be taken out of the way.*

> *8 - And then shall that Wicked be revealed, whom the LORD shall consume with the spirit of his mouth, and shall destroy with the brightness of his coming:*

I have asserted above that the position held by the son of perdition is illegitimate. Consider how verse 7 reads from the Amplified Bible:

7 - For the mystery of lawlessness (that hidden principle of rebellion against constituted authority) is already at work in the world, [but it is] restrained only until he who restrains is taken out of the way.

According to this version, the son of perdition holds his position of authority in violation of CONSTITUTED LAW. Simply put, he is in contempt of the Constitution of the Temple, and more than likely he is an unconstitutional leader.

In addition to his brief description in *2 Thessalonians 2*, his administration is described in greater detail in *Daniel 11:36-45*. There we find what his endeavors are while he is in power for his limited window of time. Each individual scripture is an informational item that stands alone, and the verses specific to him should not be read as sequential events following one right after the other. Some of the verses happen concurrently, while others take place at varying times. Based on our study thus far, I will attempt to organize them in the order in which they will play out on a timeline.

The first step for the son of perdition is to come to power. This is detailed in verse 45; the last verse of the passage.

Daniel 11:

45 - And he shall plant the tabernacles of his palace between the seas in the glorious holy mountain; yet he shall come to his end, and none shall help him.

This verse marks his first step and final step. It is a summary of his beginning and his end. For now we will focus on the beginning aspect of his reign. Where does he have his office? In the glorious holy mountain located between two seas. We'll discuss this mountain in greater detail in the next two chapters of study. Suffice it to say for now that this sounds like a pretty nice place; a place set aside by God and for God's glory, from sea to shining sea. It is the Temple that the son of perdition is interested in, and he does not have dominion over a separate kingdom. He does not have the capacity to create anything that emanates blessing, he just wants to steal it and redistribute the Temple's wealth according to his liking. His interest is in infiltrating the Kingdom of Heaven . . . Ammarica . . . with the intent of subverting it and destroying it. And I am certain he has a considerable following as seen by his capacity to incite an uprising in _Revelation 12_. There is a great falling away sponsored by a spirit of envy, deception, subversion, theft, and treason WITHIN the Kingdom. But in spite of his influence and illegal hold on power, the son of perdition will fall!

But not immediately. For a time, he will prosper, as seen in the next sequence:

> _36 - And the king shall do according to his will; and he shall exalt himself, and magnify himself above every god, and shall speak marvellous things against the God of gods, and shall prosper till the indignation be accomplished: for that that is determined shall be done._

The son of perdition is a narcissist who views himself as the people's messiah. For a nation who has thumbed its nose at the constituted laws of God, it is fitting that God will allow the son of perdition to thumb his nose at the constituted laws of the Temple. For a season.

> _37 - Neither shall he regard the God of his fathers, nor the desire of women, nor regard any god: for he shall magnify himself above all._

The son of perdition exhibits no allegiance to the Judeo-Christian God of the culture of the Temple. Many scholars agree that he will probably favor homosexual agendas in his administration. Additionally, he may be sympathetic to foreign religions that do not honor the dignity of women. The most notable religion in that category is Islam.

> _38 - But in his estate shall he honour the God of forces: and a god whom his fathers knew not shall he honour with gold, and silver, and with precious stones, and pleasant things._

Once again Islam is suspect as the god of forces. Islam is involved in every major conflict around the globe today, and it manages and converts everything through force. This is not a god historically embraced by our forefathers. President Thomas Jefferson went to war against it, and the Marine Hymn was inspired by our early battles against Islamic terror. From the halls of Montezuma to the shores of Tripoli. This song was not inspired by a war with the Girl Scouts; it was inspired by the Barbary Wars with Islam. But when the son of perdition gets into power he will favor it, enable it, and honor it with finances. The result seen in the next verse would make our forefathers turn over in their graves.

> *39 - Thus shall he do in the most strong holds with a strange god, whom he shall acknowledge and increase with glory: and he shall cause them to rule over many, and shall divide the land for gain.*

His support of Islam will enable it to gain influence, even to the extent that it exerts authority over the people. Here is a picture of Sharia law in the courts. This strange god and law have no place in our land until the son of perdition comes to power. When he does, Sharia will advance.

When we consider the statement about him dividing the land, it speaks of two things. First, there's the dividing of the House of Judah. He will probably be a proponent of a two-state solution, and will favor a Palestinian state in the land that God granted to Judah. Regarding the House of Israel, he will likely disdain our borders in favor of global concepts. He is in blatant contempt of the covenant God made with Israel as it relates to their land-grants. God ordained Israel's colonialism, and the son of perdition detests it. Border assignments for the Israelite people were given under the Abrahamic covenant. They predate both the Mosaic covenant and the New Covenant, and are upheld through both. *Galatians 3:15-17* states that if the covenant is confirmed (which it was) it cannot be disannulled or revised. Even the creation of an additional covenant some 430 years later did not alter the promises God gave to Abraham's seed. The promises were binding, and the land-grants were secured between God and Abraham. Mohammed does not have a vote. Feel-good Christians don't even have a vote. This is why Paul states in *Acts 17:26* that God has made all nations of men *"to dwell on all the face of the earth, and hath determined the times before appointed, and the bounds of their habitation"*. Borders are determined by God, and they were determined before either the New Testament or the Old. America is a sovereign nation with borders framed by God's promises to Ephraim. Yet the global agenda seeks to redefine us as a concept without borders. This is promulgated with the sole intent of controlling us. Their poster child in the Oval Office has no interest in either the House of Israel or the House of Judah maintaining ownership of their lands, and both of his policies only serve to weaken them. For the son of perdition it does not matter. In his world, his position of power is all about self-discovery, personal gain, and contempt for the Christ culture. Jumping ahead now a few verses, we find that he has some peculiar interests in the Middle East and Africa.

> *42 - He shall stretch forth his hand also upon the countries: and the land of Egypt shall not escape.*

First of all, he is responsible for some kind of coup or overthrow in Egypt in the last days.

> *43 - But he shall have power over the treasures of gold and of silver, and over all the precious things of Egypt: and the Libyans and the Ethiopians shall be at his steps.*

Additionally he has a special interest in the precious things of Egypt, Libya, and Ethiopia. One can speculate that the precious things are oil, but this we know; his focus will be on controlling Egypt, Libya, and Ethiopia. That said, he will probably engage politically and militarily in all three theaters to accomplish his endeavors. For the House of Judah, this means they will be surrounded by his minions, and it sets the stage for their suffering in *Revelation 11*. For the House of Israel, these would be unconstitutional engagements which bleed off dollars and further weaken them. He will make his play for these nations while sitting as an unconstitutional leader within the Temple. So when you see an unconstitutional leader open up military and political fronts in these three countries, it would be wise for you to pay attention. The son of perdition is being revealed. Finally, there is *verse 40*:

> *40 - And at the time of the end shall the king of the south push at him: and the king of the north shall come against him like a whirlwind, with chariots, and with horsemen, and with many ships; and he shall enter into the countries, and shall overflow and pass over.*

Here it appears that the son of perdition is the one in power when Gog and Magog make their move. If the Manchild has been taken out, and he refuses to relinquish power, this fits. Someone, however, may wonder why Gog and Magog would attack if he is the poster child of their agenda. First of all, they may read the resolve of the woman and know that their boy has no lasting support. This is their last best chance, and in that scenario he becomes expendable. Just like Judas was expendable to the Pharisees. I don't know for sure how this will play out, but as we move forward in this chapter of study you will understand that he is the Judas being used by the Beast system to gain inroads into the Temple. His rise to power and his agenda are precursors to *Daniel 12*, for according to *Daniel 12:1* the final 3½ year conflict begins "at that time" when his administration is doing these things. We want to know who he is.

Names carry meaning. Based on his name as the son of perdition, we discover that his rebellion and nature are just like Judas who betrayed Christ. We know this because Jesus also refers to Judas as a son of perdition in *John 17:12*. The ONLY places in scripture where the terms "son of perdition" are used are to describe Judas . . . and this last day usurper in the Temple of God. They must have the same nature and tactics given their identical titles. So if we want to know more about the last day son of perdition, a study of Judas becomes necessary. Consider Judas' true colors as revealed in the Gospel of John.

John 12:

> *3 - Then took Mary a pound of ointment of spikenard, very costly, and anointed the feet of Jesus, and wiped his feet with her hair: and the house was filled with the odour of the ointment.*

> *4 - Then saith one of his disciples, Judas Iscariot, Simon's son, which should betray him,*

> *5 - Why was not this ointment sold for three hundred pence, and given to the poor?*

> *6 - This he said, not that he cared for the poor; but because he was a thief, and had the bag, and bare what was put therein.*

> *7 - Then said Jesus, Let her alone: against the day of my burying hath she kept this.*

8 - For the poor always ye have with you; but me ye have not always.

A few things stand out in this passage. First we discover that the original son of perdition was intent on stealing from the public treasury. In effect, that is what "the bag" represented in verse 6. It was the treasury for the little culture of Christ consisting of 12 disciples. But to accomplish his theft, he had to cloak it in legitimacy so it would not be seen for what it really was. He couldn't just come out of the closet and declare himself to be a thief. He had to spin himself as a champion for the poor at the expense of the Christ culture, and hope that nobody noticed. So he cloaked his redistribution-of-wealth policy under the guise of social justice. His interest was not in the Christ-centered culture of his surroundings, for he disdained the elevation of Jesus to a place of preeminence. As soon as Christ put him in his place and told him to leave the woman alone, his little entitlement scheme came to an abrupt end. He promptly went and sold out to the enemy, and opened up the door for them to do their dirty deeds. Judas was the one they had been waiting for. With Judas being the forerunner to the last day son of perdition, this is a microscopic view of :

- Redistribution of wealth from the treasury . . .
- Cloaked as social justice and entitlements . . .
- Rooted in greed and a thirst for power . . .
- Promoted by a thief . . .
- In a culture of Christ consisting of 12 disciples.

Today's "progressives" have a word for this kind of evil; they call it "compassion". But it is driven by a spirit of envy, subversion, and treachery; yet sold as a noble endeavor. Will the last day usurper have the same nature and use the same tactics as that of his predecessor?

In other words, could the conflict of *Revelation 12* be initiated by the last day son of perdition and his handlers? As he sits as an unconstitutional leader in the seat of power, in the Executive branch, will he sell out to the other side? Will his final betrayal come on the heels of his pet entitlement program being smacked down in favor of honoring the culture of Christ? What Judas did in *John 12* is just a microscopic view of what the last day son of perdition will do on a macro level. His impetus will be the redistribution of wealth from the treasury . . . cloaked as social justice and entitlements . . . rooted in greed and a thirst for power . . . promoted by a thief . . . in a culture of Christ consisting not of 12 disciples, but of the 12 tribes of Israel. It is the same story on a much larger scale. All it would take is a Supreme Court ruling shutting his theft down, and he would be livid enough to sell out the entire culture to the enemy. In a state of disdain for the Christ culture, he will open the door to her enemies who wish to destroy her. Remember this about Judas; he himself did not launch the attack on Christ. He just opened the door to those who wanted to do it, and with a kiss he betrayed that which he should have been loyal to. This is the nature of the son of doom, loss, or perdition.

Here now is what we know. By the end of days, the Dragon / Beast system gains a foothold in this place called Heaven of _Revelation 12_. This place is also known as the Temple in _Revelation 11_, and we know it to be the United States of America. This is the same Temple as seen in _2 Thessalonians 2_, and it appears that the son of perdition is Commander in Chief in VIOLATION OF THE CONSTITUTION. If he is anything like his predecessor, he wants to steal from the Christ-centered culture of the Temple, or redistribute its wealth. In the process, he has no intention of honoring the Christ-centered culture of the Temple because he disdains the aroma of Christ. Destroying it is not a problem in his mind. So he will work to advance HIS agenda in the name of social justice and entitlements, and will spin himself as a champion for the poor at the expense of the Christian culture. The non-discerning will swallow it hook, line, and sinker.

The good news is that according to _2 Thessalonians 2_ he is revealed as the usurper that he is, and thrown down! The not so good news is that according to _Revelation 12_, these events will precipitate:

- An uprising by his followers within America . . .
- Which coincides with the invasion detailed in _Ezekiel 38_ . . .
- And many will fight to the death to finally liberate our land.

The Temple will be cleansed and sealed, but the global restraint against evil abroad will be removed. The Beast will no longer be muzzled, and this will be the beginning of great tribulation for the entire world. Except within the Temple. The Beast's secondary target will be the House of

Judah, and it will throw everything it has against this other half of the Kingdom of Israel.

To get a better view of how this will develop, a foundational understanding of how evil and usurpation work together is necessary. To accomplish that, let's focus our attention on the nature of satan himself. The usurper-in-chief is inspiring this last day rebellion in the Temple, and there is a lot of ground yet to be covered in this chapter of study. We turn now to the book of _Isaiah_, where we see satan undertaking this same endeavor.

Isaiah 14:

> _12 - How art thou fallen from heaven, O Lucifer, son of the morning! how art thou cut down to the ground, which didst weaken the nations!_

> _13 - For thou hast said in thine heart, I will ascend into heaven, I will exalt my throne above the stars of God: I will sit also upon the mount of the congregation, in the sides of the north:_

> _14 - I will ascend above the heights of the clouds; I will be like the most High._

> _15 - Yet thou shalt be brought down to hell, to the sides of the pit._

When we understand that this is satan himself in his endeavor to overthrow literal heaven, we can also conclude that this took place long before our time. It probably occurred in a very literal sense sometime before the creation of Adam and Eve in the Garden of Eden. Yet there are elements in here indicating that it is a single prophecy with a dual fulfillment. This is something that played out in the spiritual realm which we cannot see, and has yet to play out in the earthly realm which we can see. It began in the heavenly realm, and as I've pointed out, that aspect of the prophecy is now history. But it also includes an earthly realm indicated by Lucifer's intent to sit _also_ (round 2) upon the "_mount of the congregation, in the sides of the north_". Why do I connect that to some earthly fulfillment? _Psalm 48:1-2_ states that an earthly entity called Zion is the mountain of God's holiness, on the sides of the north. It reads as follows.

Psalm 48:

> *1 - Great is the LORD, and greatly to be praised in the city of our God, in the mountain of his holiness.*

> *2 - Beautiful for situation, the joy of the whole earth, is mount Zion, on the sides of the north, the city of the great King.*

This earthly entity that David is describing bears significant resemblance to the entity satan wants to overthrow in *Isaiah 14*. A few verses further in *Psalm 48* show David giving more detail about this entity he calls Zion:

> *6 - Fear took hold upon them there, and pain, as of a woman in travail.*

This sounds like the birth of the Manchild in *Revelation 12*. In *Revelation 12* she's called the Woman. Here she's called Zion.

> *9 - We have thought of thy lovingkindness, O God, in the midst of thy temple.*

In this verse, Zion, the mountain of God's holiness, is called the Temple. When we connect all the different yet corresponding labels assigned to this same people, the train of thought would look like this:

- The mount of the congregation in *Isaiah 14* . . .
- Is Zion in *Psalms 48* . . .
- Also referred to as the Temple in *Psalms 48:9* . . .
- Which is the same Temple in *Revelation 11* . . .
- Which is the Woman of *Revelation 12* . . .
- Which we know is the House of Israel . . .
- Which we know is America.
- The mount of the congregation = Zion = the Temple = the Woman = the House of Israel = America.

All of these different labels or names correspond to the same people group; the House of Israel. If that logic train is a stretch, weigh it against the Word of God. *Amos 6:1* states "*Woe to them that are at ease in Zion, and trust in the mountain of Samaria,* (her government) *which are named chief of the nations, to whom the house of Israel came!*" This verse says a mouthful about her seat of power, her government, her people's misplaced trust in big government and her military prowess, and her rise as a superpower. I point it out because it expressly links the House of Israel to Zion. It validates the train of thought detailed above. Zion becomes a strong nation in the end of days, and the House of Israel gathers to her.

Historically, Zion existed in the Old Testament as the "City of David". Prophetically however, Zion is also revealed to be something fresh and new that is built in the last days. In *Micah 4* Zion is established as a nation IN THE LAST DAYS. In *Joel 2* Zion is attacked by invaders IN THE LAST DAYS. In both cases Zion is an earthly entity complete with land holdings. And regardless of the timing in which it is used in scripture, Zion is always connected to the House of Israel. Zion is the House of Israel set aside for God's glory, combined with people drawn into that "Christ culture". It is spiritual in origin, yet physical in expression. It is the Kingdom of Heaven on earth. Historically, when the House of Israel fell into sin and dispersed, Zion ceased to exist. In the last days, when the House of Israel would gather under Christ, Zion would re-form. But it would be on a larger scale. It would no longer be the "City of David", it would be the "Mountain of the house of the LORD". This is the story told in *Micah 4*, and you can rest assured we will discuss this in detail in the chapters ahead.

To reiterate, Zion is not just a concept or spiritual belief. And it is not the House of Judah. It must be a viable people group distinct from the Jews, and existing in the here and now. So where do we find all the ingredients of this coming together? In the United States of America! This is the only nation in history, built by the church and the House of Israel that qualifies for the descriptions of Zion given by David in *Psalm 48*. It is the mountain of the LORD, the mount of the congregation in the sides of the north. And this is the nation that satan "*also*" intends to reign over as seen in *Isaiah 14*.

As a spirit being, however, he cannot do that directly like he tried in literal heaven. He must do it through his emissary, which happens to be the son of perdition. This is the scenario seen in *2 Thessalonians 2* and quite possibly a precursor to the big battle in *Revelation 12*. The battle is for government within the Temple! The key position is that of Commander in Chief. In *2 Thessalonians 2*, satan is shown to usurp that position for a season through his emissary, the son of perdition. Christian America has served as a restrainer of evil around the world, and the enemy wants that restraint removed. David alludes to this endeavor and rise of evil over Zion in *Psalms 2*. This is yet one more passage referring to Zion, and we'll flesh out the details as we read it through.

Psalms 2:

> *1 - Why do the heathen rage, and the people imagine a vain thing?*

What are they imagining? We're about to find out.

> *2 - The kings of the earth set themselves, and the rulers take counsel together, against the LORD, and against his anointed, saying,*

> *3 - Let us break their bands asunder, and cast away their cords from us.*

The kings of the earth are conspiring against the House of Israel under God to break off their restraint. After all, Christian America has held them back for too long, and they are tired of our dominance and the Christ-centered culture of the nation. They prefer the model of Judas. But this is a comedy show for God.

> *4 - He that sitteth in the heavens shall laugh: the LORD shall have them in derision.*

> *5 - Then shall he speak unto them in his wrath, and vex them in his sore displeasure.*

> *6 - Yet have I set my king upon my holy hill of Zion.*

Apparently, part of their conspiring involves taking possession of the Executive branch of Zion. It has never been God's intent for anyone other than the seed of David to reign over the House of Israel, in spite of their division with the House of Judah. Before continuing with *Psalms 2*, consider the words of Jeremiah. *Jeremiah 33:17* says *For thus saith the LORD; David shall never want a man to sit upon the throne of the house of*

Israel. Sorry globalists, America's leader comes from the tribe of Judah, and this is why EVERY President to occupy the Oval Office was connected to David's royal lineage through the lineage of their father. God has kept His Word to David's seed and the House of Israel, and the kings of the earth want to overthrow God's covenant with them. They attempt to do that by usurping the provisions of the covenant and placing a leader in power that has a different father than David. But the LORD reiterates His promise to David in *Psalms 2*:

> *7 - I will declare the decree: the LORD hath said unto me (David), Thou art my Son; this day have I begotten thee.*

> *8 - Ask of me, and I shall give thee the heathen for thine inheritance, and the uttermost parts of the earth for thy possession.*

Ultimately this speaks of Christ, but until His return it applies to David's seed which lives on and reigns over the House of Israel in the uttermost parts of the earth. Hence, the rise of the Manchild as seen in the next verse:

> *9 - Thou shalt break them with a rod of iron; thou shalt dash them in pieces like a potter's vessel.*

The battle for the Oval Office is now under way. The Manchild is rising, and there is no compromise in his soul. And through it all, God's message to the global community remains constant:

> *10 - Be wise now therefore, O ye kings: be instructed, ye judges of the earth.*

> *11 - Serve the LORD with fear, and rejoice with trembling.*

> *12 - Kiss the Son, lest he be angry, and ye perish from the way, when his wrath is kindled but a little. Blessed are all they that put their trust in him.*

God's plan is for the seed of David to rule over the House of Israel. Globalists need to kiss up to that idea and comply with it. You will only be blessed when you bless what God blesses, and curse what He curses. There are no shortcuts. So in short, *Psalms 2* is all about the heathen trying to bring about change they can believe in, in the Temple of God where they do not belong!

With these things in mind, our next stop is in *Luke 10*. Before we read a key verse there, remember that Jesus was the Word made flesh, and was in existence before the earth took on physical form. Since He is God revealed through the Son, He was witness to the heavenly rebellion of *Isaiah 14* before the creation of the world. As of today it has yet to play out on earth, but at some point it must in the end of days. Remember, it is a single prophecy with a dual fulfillment. Listen carefully to how Jesus described the usurpation and casting down of satan in *Luke*.

Luke 10:18 - And Jesus said unto them, I beheld Satan as lightning fall from heaven.

This passage correlates with satan's endeavors and subsequent fall as detailed in *Isaiah 14*. Jesus is describing to His disciples the historical aspect of that event which took place in the spiritual realm which we cannot see. But could He also be revealing something regarding satan's future play against the House of Israel as seen in *Isaiah 14*? Could he be revealing something about the son of perdition who usurps the throne in the Temple on earth in the last days? Only time will tell for certain, but consider the following. These words of Jesus are written in Greek, and translated into English. However, it is likely that Jesus would have spoken these words in Aramaic; the most ancient form of Hebrew. Hebrew has always been the language of the Jewish people, and as most Bible students know the Old Testament was written in Hebrew. If a Jewish Rabbi would speak these words today, he would speak them in Hebrew. And since Hebrew is Hebrew, the phrase would sound the same as how Jesus said it in His time. What would this sound like if you stated it in the Hebrew tongue? To answer the question, refer to a Bible study tool that many Christians have access to either in book form or through an online version on the Internet; it's called Strong's Hebrew Dictionary and Concordance. This is a work that you can use to validate what I write, and it is independent of any influence on my part. It is also something that was first published in the 1800's, so it is free of all modern politics.

Jesus describes satan's fall in *Isaiah 14* as one being like lightning from the heavens. Let's begin with the word "lightning". The Hebrew root word for lightning is indexed in the Strong's Concordance as word 1299. It is recorded as follows:

<u>1299 - A primitive root; to lighten (lightning) to cast forth.</u>

It is the Hebrew word Baraq, pronounced as baw-rak. The other Hebrew word related to Baraq is indexed as word 1300. It is similar, and it is recorded in <u>Strong's Concordance</u> as follows:

<u>1300 - From baraq; lightning, by analogy, a gleam; a flashing sword, bright, glittering, lightning—Baraq (baw-rawk).</u>

It is essentially the same word, only pronounced a little differently. It is pronounced as baw-rawk. So the Hebrew word meaning to cast forth as lightning is Baw-rak or Baw-rawk.

Next, let's look at the word "heights" or "heaven". After all, satan's intention in *Isaiah 14* is to ascend above the heights of the clouds, or in a symbolic sense to ascend into heaven. This is where he intends to sit, and it is from this position that he falls like lightning. Once again, we reference the <u>Strong's Concordance</u>. The Hebrew word used in this text to describe the place from which he falls is indexed as word 1116. It is defined as follows:

<u>1116 - From an unused root (meaning to be high); an elevation, height, high place.</u>

It is the Hebrew word Bamah, pronounced as bam-maw.

The Hebrew language has no vowels in it, and consonants are often joined together with a conjunction. Joining the two concepts of "falling like lightning" and "from the heights" may include a vowel-like sounding conjunction of "U" or "O", and in the Hebrew the complete phrase would sound something like this; "Baraq O Bamah" or "Baraq U Bamah". Literally translated in English, it means "falling like lightning from the heights" or "Heaven".

As Jesus spoke these words 2,000 years ago to describe satan's historical play at usurping the throne of God, and quite possibly pointing to satan's future aspirations against the House of Israel as detailed in _Isaiah 14_, an English / Hebrew hybrid of _Luke 10:18_ would have sounded something like this; "I saw satan as baraq o bamah" or "I saw satan fall like lightning from the heights". In the days ahead, will America witness the son of perdition as "baraq o bamah"? If yes, you and I are almost out of "normal" time and the final battle looms. Until we know for certain, consider the Word of God given to Moses for national Israel, which is captured in _Deuteronomy 28_.

Deuteronomy 28:

> _1 - And it shall some to pass, if thou shalt hearken diligently unto the voice of the Lord they God, to observe and to do all his commandments which I command thee this day, that the Lord thy God will set thee on high above all nations of the earth:_

> _2 - And all these blessings shall come on thee, and overtake thee, if thou shalt hearken unto the voice of the Lord thy God._

Here is a promise given to our nation that we will be blessed by God, simply by placing His law central to our culture. This passage is not about how to build a family, business, or church. It is not even about how to attain individual salvation. It is about how we the Saxons are to build our nation. If we want to sing God bless America as a prayer and expect God to honor it, America should focus her efforts on obedience to God. There are no shortcuts to God's blessing. If we obey Him, we can expect the blessings of God to chase us and overtake our nation! These blessings are listed from verse 3 to verse 14 of _Deuteronomy 28_, and they are something I want for America.

However, the chapter does not end there. Verse 15 picks up the national charter with these words:

> _15 - But it shall come to pass, if thou wilt not hearken unto the voice of the Lord they God, to observe to do all his commandments and his statutes which I command thee this day; that all these curses shall come upon thee, and overtake thee:_

Verse 16 through verse 68 then detail the "curses" which God will bring upon America as a result of it turning away from Him. In light of our study on the son of perdition, I want to quickly focus on three of them.

43 - The stranger that is within thee shall get up above the very high; and thou shalt come down very low.

Progressives have hailed the election of Barack Obama as a national triumph. But according to God's Word, it was a national tragedy. The stranger in Israel is the foreigner, and one without the birth certificate. He is not a natural born citizen, and his rise to power over Israel is an indication they are coming into judgment because of their national disobedience. This verse certainly applies to both topics of illegal aliens in general, and a usurper in the Oval Office. Applying it to the latter, that stranger would have no affinity for Israel and he would disdain their laws, their constitution, their culture and their God. Our forefathers understood this danger and made constitutional assurances that such a man would never come to power. His entire work would be to enslave the people of God, and one of his methods is detailed in the next verse.

44 - He shall lend to thee, and thou shalt not lend to him: he shall be the head, and thou shalt be the tail.

In a general sense, God is showing Israel that if they choose a path of disobedience they will be in debt to foreign nations. Nations like China. Increased debt is not a sign of God's blessing; it is a sign of God's disapproval with Israel. If we apply this verse to the stranger in the Oval Office, that foreigner will likely increase the debt load to the point that the nation cannot recover. He is not doing it to help the Saxons; he is doing it to bury them. Barack Obama has committed America to more debt in his administration than all previous administrations from George Washington to George Bush COMBINED. Do you see that as irony, or is it a deliberate attempt to enslave us through debt? Either way, it is God telling us that we have turned away from Him. But wait there's more . . .

49 - The Lord shall bring a nation against thee from far, from the end of the earth, as swift as the eagle flieth; a nation whose tongue thou shalt not understand;

50 - A nation of fierce countenance, which shall not regard the person of the old, nor shew favour to the young:

51 - And he shall eat the fruit of thy cattle, and the fruit of thy land, until thou be destroyed: which also shall not leave thee either corn, wine, or oil, or the increase of thy kine, or flocks of they sheep, until he have destroyed thee.

Or as Ezekiel states it, Gog and Magog will attack the House of Israel to "*. . . take a spoil, and to take a prey; to turn thine hand upon the desolate places that are now inhabited, and upon the people that are gathered out of the nations, which have gotten cattle and goods, that dwell in the midst of the land*". God warns the House of Israel that these three things will happen in succession when they turn away from God. Two of them are occurring as we speak, and one is knocking at the door. Can it get any more clear?

Many get the feeling that America is but a stepping stone for Barack Obama's ambitions. Is he THE "baraq o bamah" of scripture that usurps the throne in the Temple illegally? That remains to be seen, and only time will tell. Everything will become evident soon enough. But his spirit and actions are consistent with that of the Beast system, and the first son of perdition. With the assistance of the legal system, the courts, the kings of the earth, and an ambivalent law enforcement community he continues to perpetuate the greatest act of fraud ever committed against our nation. Forensic analysis has proven his Certificate of Live Birth to be an outright fraud, yet his lawlessness is allowed to prosper by those who turn a blind eye. Can you remember a time in history when a Commander in Chief could hide his records, come from nowhere, falsify his eligibility, present a poorly rendered fraud to the public, and pass it all off with ease? If his Birth Certificate is a fraud, he is likely the Commander in Chief in violation of the Constitution. If he is deposed of his power through impeachment, rest assured it will spark a *Revelation 12* uprising by his followers. The entire presidency and every bill signed into law since January 2009 would be rendered invalid, and a Constitutional crisis of extreme magnitude would ensue. The labor pains involved in birthing a legitimate leader of the free world would be unparalleled. It would be uncharted waters for America, and any hint of a return to strict Constitutional nationalism would send the Dragon into a tizzy. It has no intentions of relinquishing its hold on the _third part of the stars of heaven_. If it plays out this way, many Israelites who have defected to the side of evil, or fallen away, will side with the Dragon. The atmosphere would be ripe for war and there would be no middle ground. You would either be for the Woman, or for the Dragon; and a fight over Mr. Falling-Like-Lightning-From-The-Heights' demise and the birth of the Manchild would be unavoidable. Gog and Magog will be waiting in the wings licking their chops. All they need is a Judas.

I understand this is a lot to process, but that is of little consequence right now. The bigger issue is that we need to continually challenge our preconceived notions with the authority of God's Word. If we fail to do that, we can be easily blinded to the fulfillment of prophecy. It happened with the Pharisees in their quest to maintain the status quo, and it can happen to us too. We can easily miss what is happening right before our eyes unless we normalize the mysteries of prophecy. In the meantime, as we watch and pray, a corrupt machine is stealing from the treasury of the Temple to redistribute its wealth in unprecedented fashion. National debt equates to theft from future generations, and as stated earlier this administration has run up a tab greater than all other administrations combined. The treasury is being emptied just as the son of perdition would want. Barack Obama has no intention of honoring the Christ-centered culture of the Temple because he disdains its colonial reach which was ordained by God. Destroying it is not a problem in his mind. So he advances his agenda of destruction in the name of social justice and entitlements, and spins himself as a champion for the poor at the expense of the Christian culture. It is an effective cloak for thievery, and the non-discerning have swallowed it hook, line, and sinker. From his nomination in the highest state of the nation . . . the mountain state of Colorado . . . in the Mile High city of the same (Denver) . . . to his usurpation as an unconstitutional leader of our land, he has shown his true colors. He covets the mountain of the LORD, which is detailed in our next chapter of study.

CHAPTER 8

The Mountain of the LORD

As we launch out into other passages of scripture, we must ask one simple question: Will it blend? Does it blend with the body of knowledge we have acquired thus far? Our next passage of scripture details the establishment of Zion in the last days, and we must examine it from this perspective. Does it blend with everything we have learned to this point? If it tells a different story, we must figure out where we are in error in our interpretations. Perhaps it is speaking of a different time period. Perhaps it tells an entirely different story of the time period we are studying. But to reiterate, if it tells a different story, we must figure out how to reconcile our knowledge which can be fallible, with the unerring Word of God. If it tells the same story, we are on the right track. As we open up a new text, our position leading up to this chapter will be put to the test. And frankly, it should be, because we do not want to settle for anything other than the truth, the whole truth, and nothing but the truth. If our position is solid, then other passages of scripture will blend perfectly with the layers previously discussed. Up next is _Micah 4_.

Before we begin, remember what was stated about Zion in the scripture. Zion existed in the Old Testament as the City of David, yet it is also shown to be something fresh and new that is built in the last days. In its inception, it was a city. In the last days, it is the mountain of the LORD. It is much larger. And regardless of its usage, it is always connected to the House of Israel. When they left Palestine, Zion ceased to exist. Hence it must be rebuilt in the last days because this is the time period when the whole House of Israel will reassemble as one nation under God in one location. From our previous study we've seen David already describe it as beautiful for situation (or a beautiful location and land) . . . the joy of the whole earth . . . on the sides of the north (north Ommerike) . . . the house of

God. For the sake of our study, we will focus on the last day development of Zion because this is the piece satan wants to preside over through his emissary, the son of perdition. Let's work through *Micah 4* verse by verse to see what it reveals.

Micah 4:

> *1 - But in the last days it shall come to pass, that the mountain of the house of the LORD shall be established in the top of the mountains, and it shall be exalted above the hills; and people shall flow unto it.*

On the scale of human history, the time period for the fulfillment of this chapter is placed "in the last days". *Daniel 12:4* describes the last days as a time when many shall run "*to and fro and knowledge shall be increased*". With the marvels of modern transportation and technology, we have sufficient evidence to conclude that we live in the last days. We live in the period of time when this passage is being fulfilled. It is speaking of right now.

Notice that Micah immediately labels this grand work of God as a mountain. Is this the "*mount of the congregation*" in *Isaiah 14*? Is it "*mount Zion*" as mentioned in *Psalm 48*? One would think so, unless of course the prophets are seeing different mountains. I can say with all assurance that mountains in scripture are often symbolic references to governments. The book of *Daniel* provides clarity on this, and to that end *Daniel 2:34-35* reads as follows:

Daniel 2:

> *34 - Thou sawest till that a stone was cut out without hands, which smote the image upon his feet that were of iron and clay, and brake them to pieces.*

> *35 - Then was the iron, the clay, the brass, the silver, and the gold, broken to pieces together, and became like the chaff of the summer threshingfloors; and the wind carried them away, that no place was found for them: and the stone that smote the image became a great mountain, and filled the whole earth.*

This describes God's government as established in the last days; His "*mountain*". This is the Kingdom OF Heaven on earth, not the Kingdom IN Heaven that is beyond the realm of human sight. Its manifestation is in the same fashion as Kingdoms that preceded it, not in a fashion invisible to the eye. But while other Kingdoms on earth have come and gone, the final one will not and it is described as God's mountain. This is reiterated later in the same chapter.

Daniel 2:

> *44 - And in the days of these kings shall the God of heaven set up a kingdom, which shall never be destroyed: and the kingdom shall not be left to other people, but it shall break in pieces and consume all these kingdoms, and it shall stand for ever.*

> *45 - Forasmuch as thou sawest that the stone was cut out of the mountain without hands, and that it brake in pieces the iron, the brass, the clay, the silver, and the gold; the great God hath made known to the king what shall come to pass hereafter: and the dream is certain, and the interpretation thereof sure.*

Since God is not going away, neither will His Kingdom on earth. He is subservient to no man, and His Kingdom is subservient to none other than Himself. This mountain will dominate the global community *in the last days.*

Micah 4:1 is a short verse, but it says a mouthful. Here is what we know from it alone; the mountain of the house of the Lord is God's premiere work established on earth in the last days. This will truly be known as one nation under God, and He will favor and bless this nation above all others. It will be exalted above all nations, and people will beat the doors down to get IN to her. Some will do it legally; others will not. Regardless of how they approach this work of God, people want to be a part of her because this mountain will be seen by the global community as the land of opportunity and blessing. Let's read forward as the rest of this passage builds on this thought.

2a—And many nations shall come, and say, Come, and let us go up to the mountain of the LORD, and to the house of the God of Jacob . . .

Here is firm evidence that the mountain of the LORD is connected to the house of the God of Jacob. Jacob is Israel, so this is referring to either the House of Israel or the House of Judah. And people want to be a part of her in the last days. The result is that whichever Kingdom she is, the mountain of the LORD will be a melting pot of many nationalities. The answer as to which Kingdom this is begins to show up in the next verse.

2b— . . . and he will teach us of his ways, and we will walk in his paths . . .

As people flock to this nation conceived in the courts of heaven, they will enter a place that has built its national life on the precepts of Jesus Christ! The global community will recognize this as the central nation for the teaching of God's ways. Today that is not Judaism, it is Christianity. Anyone can come to the mountain of the Lord and freely be taught of Christ's ways, probably in one of her many churches that dot the landscape. This begins to reveal to us that this is not the House of Judah, but instead the House of Israel. God has not called the church to go the way of the Jew, but He has called the Jew to go the way of the cross. This mountain has been built on the way of the cross. We don't have her name yet, but I suspect you know where this is going. Let's see if the Word of God confirms our suspicions.

2c— . . . for the law shall go forth of Zion, and the word of the LORD from Jerusalem.

This is Zion. This is not IN ancient Jerusalem; this is ZION which has built her national life on the law that came forth FROM Jerusalem. If you skim this verse and don't study the wording, it's easy to assume the container for Zion is ancient Jerusalem. In this passage Jerusalem is not Zion's container; it is Zion's inspiration. It is the origination point for what ZION is now carrying. The law transferred FROM Jerusalem . . . to be carried OF (or by) Zion. This was foretold by Jesus Himself in *Matthew*.

Matthew 21:

> *43 - Therefore say I unto you (Judah), The kingdom of God shall be taken from you (Judah), and given to a nation bringing forth the fruits thereof.*

> *44 - And whosoever shall fall on this stone shall be broken: but on whomsoever it shall fall, it will grind him to powder.*

The commission of the stone Kingdom was taken from Judah and given to another nation. The stone Kingdom that eventually becomes a mountain would be built by a nation other than Judah. She is called Zion in scripture, and we know it is connected to the House of Israel.

For the sake of clarity, I will provide you with one more bit of proof. If you insist on shoe-horning this passage into ancient and literal Jerusalem, you have a problem. The problem is trying to reconcile this passage with *Revelation 11:8*. There we see God has a different last day name for literal Jerusalem, and it is that of "*Sodom and Egypt*". In the last days, it cannot be both titles applying to the same people group at the same time. In the last days, literal Jerusalem is either Zion or it is Sodom and Egypt. We know it to be the latter because the House of Judah was decreed as desolate in *Matthew* because they rejected Christ.

Matthew 23:

> *37 - O Jerusalem, Jerusalem, thou that killest the prophets, and stonest them which are sent unto thee, how often would I have gathered thy children together, even as a hen gathereth her chickens under her wings, and ye would not!*

> *38 - Behold, your house (the House of Judah) is left unto you desolate.*

> *39 - For I say unto you, Ye shall not see me henceforth, till ye shall say, Blessed is he that cometh in the name of the LORD.*

The House of Judah will be desolate until they say "*blessed is He who comes in the Name of the LORD*", and that will not happen until just prior to

Christ's return. The call to Judah is that they must embrace the Messiah! And just as the Temple is cleansed through judgment, so Judah too . . . the Outer Court . . . will be cleansed through great tribulation. They will turn to Christ before He returns!

My sole purpose in driving this home is to draw out this truth; _Micah 4_ is not referring to the House of Judah. This is Zion which David described as a beautiful land and the joy of the whole earth. This is the nation the son of perdition wants to preside over, and will for a time. This is the fullest expression of what God birthed FROM Jerusalem in _Acts 2_. Do we find these things in the House of Judah? Or do we find them in the House of Israel today? These are characteristics of the House of Israel, or America. We know she is the only nation to be built from the ground up upon the laws of God that originated FROM Jerusalem. Let's continue in _Micah 4_ to see what God does in and through Zion. If this is America, everything else describing Zion must blend with who we are as a people.

> _3 - And he shall judge among many people, and rebuke strong nations afar off; and they shall beat their swords into plowshares, and their spears into pruninghooks: nation shall not lift up a sword against nation, neither shall they learn war any more._

Through the establishment of Zion, God will subdue and disarm other nations of the world. She appears to have a foreign policy that follows a pattern of conquer, disarm, declare peace, and rebuild. And while strong, she will be more interested in peace and safety than imperialism and war. The result?

> _4 - But they shall sit every man under his vine and under his fig tree; and none shall make them afraid: for the mouth of the LORD of hosts hath spoken it._

Because of her blessings and strength, she will be unafraid of anyone. Peace and safety will be the prevailing atmosphere in Zion, since she appears to be the lone superpower. This is consistent with her description as the House of Israel in _Ezekiel 38_. But wait, there's more!

5 - For all people will walk every one in the name of his god, and we will walk in the name of the LORD our God for ever and ever.

Not only will Zion be the lone superpower, but it will be a nation that embraces religious freedom. The TRUE God (capital G) will be worshipped by Micah's people (known to be Israel), and other gods (little g) will be worshipped by foreigners who have made this nation home. People true to Christ will worship God, while others will be allowed to worship their gods. This is not an endorsement of false religions; it is just a statement of fact as to what Zion will look like. It is one of her characteristics that allow us to identity her.

6 - In that day, saith the LORD, will I assemble her that halteth, and I will gather her that is driven out, and her that I have afflicted;

One of the characteristics of Zion is that it will be known as a place of asylum. Both political and religious asylum will be possible there. More specifically, "*her that halteth*" refers to the House of Judah. Her kingdom faltered, but she was never expelled from Palestine. The House of Israel however was removed from Palestine, and she is the one who was "*driven out*". The establishment of Zion begins the process of joining the House of Israel to her brother nation the House of Judah, as both people groups find refuge and safety within her borders. And though the Kingdoms are still separate in land holdings, Zion brings them together at least politically. A reunion is coming, and the next verse builds on this premise.

7 - And I will make her that halted a remnant, and her that was cast far off a strong nation: and the LORD shall reign over them in mount Zion from henceforth, even for ever.

Once again we see asylum in this passage, and it consists largely of a divided Kingdom from ages past. The "*halted*" ones become a remnant (the House of Judah), or a small group of people. The "*cast off*" ones become a strong nation (the House of Israel). The LORD will reign over BOTH houses from Zion! In other words, as Zion goes, so goes both Kingdoms. Of the Jewish state of Israel and the House of Israel! If you need proof to this end, just turn to the headlines. The greatest ally of the House of Judah is the United States of America, and everything spins on American policy. Is it any wonder that the son of perdition wants to rule her? He is deceived into thinking he can effectively nullify the covenant that God has made with both nations if he can be their King. He is compelled into his usurpation through covetousness, and the greatness of Zion is seen in her maturity in the next verse:

> *8 - And thou, O tower of the flock, the strong hold of the daughter of Zion, unto thee shall it come, even the first dominion; the kingdom shall come to the daughter of Jerusalem.*

Finally, at long last, the House of Israel becomes the nation of global dominion and Kingdom authority that it once was. It is a return to her first dominion. For the House of Israel, the word to describe them is hegemony, or uncontested prominence. This is the Stone Kingdom in *Daniel 2* that starts small in the days of other kings, but grows into a mountain in the last days.

Realistically, something of this magnitude will take time to develop. It is possible that the time frame between verse 1 and verse 8 may be a few hundred years. Maybe 400 years or so. A cumulative tally of her characteristics from all of these verses would look something like this:

Zion is:

- A multiethnic nation built on God's favor and principles.
- Blessed above all other nations in the world.
- The source of Christianity to the world.
- A conquering nation but not an occupying nation given to imperialism (she declares peace and embraces peace).
- A place where her people will be dwelling in peace and safety.
- A lone superpower.
- The gathering place for all the tribes of Israel . . . the physical and spiritual offspring of Jerusalem.
- A place of religious freedom, political and religious asylum, and a nation of dominance and Kingdom authority.
- Birthed as a nation in the last days.

This all takes place "*in the last days*", and this is the mountain of God's holiness that the son of perdition wants to rule over. So what nation is in existence RIGHT NOW that fits this description? It is the United States of America! Perhaps now we can begin to grasp the significance of a small band of people who stepped off a boat called the Mayflower in 1620. They signed our first government into existence with a document called the "Mayflower Compact" which reads in part; ". . . we whose names are underwritten . . . having undertaken for the glory of God and advancement of the Christian faith . . . a voyage to plant the first colony in Virginia . . .". Zion was under way!

Today, Islam hates Zionism. Zionism exists as colonialism under Christ, and this infuriates the Muslim and Muslim sympathizer. But America is Zionism in the flesh. Recently, Dalia Mogahed, a member of Obama's faith advisory council declared that Osama bin Laden is a revolutionary and compares him to the liberal icon Ernesto "Che" Guevara. Her position is that bin Laden was not primarily motivated by religion but by "perceptions of imperialism and oppression and humiliation". In other words, she was pointing out that bin Laden was motivated by anti-Zionism, and that inspires Obama's inner circle. Conversely, Zionism is sponsored by heaven. It was Almighty God who moved the House of Israel to establish America under God! What motivates today's Whitehouse is not what motivates God, and the two are in conflict. God will win because Zion is God's idea. For now though, let's continue forward in this passage of scripture. There is a transition coming for Zion, and the details are given in the next few verses. Will it blend with what we have already learned? Let's find out.

> *9 - Now why dost thou cry out aloud? is there no king in thee? is thy counsellor perished? for pangs have taken thee as a woman in travail.*

From a man's perspective, I would define travail as labor pains in giving birth, shouting, screaming, blood, sweat and tears. It is not pretty. At some point in this nation's history, she will have trouble producing a "king" or national leader. In today's terms, that office would be the President. Zion labors to bring forth a "king", and it also appears that he perishes. You see, Zion cannot be the universal church, because she does not wrestle with such issues. The church has a King and His name is Jesus. And this cannot be in the Millennium, because these are not millennial events and issues. In the last days, Zion will not have a President, and labor will ensue. What is Zion to do?

10a—Be in pain, and labour to bring forth, O daughter of Zion, like a woman in travail:

In this season of turmoil, Zion's King will come into office through what is described as travail. Everyone say Manchild. This is Micah's view into *Revelation 12*! This is the battle for the Oval Office, the birth of the Manchild, and his being caught up to God and His throne! And this is the window of time in which things begin to unravel in Zion. As you think back to our study of *Revelation 12*, what does the Woman do when she travails in birth, and the dragon attacks her?

10b—. . . for now shalt thou go forth out of the city, and thou shalt dwell in the field . . .

She flees to the "wilderness". It is "get out of Dodge" time as the Dragon invades, and the people flee inland to get away from his hordes. In short, this is the same story as *Revelation 12* and it is brought on through the birth of the Manchild. Everything comes to a head with the battle over the throne. Continuing onward with verse 10 we discover that the Woman is also engaged militarily somewhere else on the globe.

10c—. . . and thou shalt go even to Babylon; there shalt thou be delivered; there the LORD shall redeem thee from the hand of thine enemies.

During this time, Zion will be embroiled in the affairs of Babylon in the name of delivering itself from its enemies. Ancient Babylon is known today as Iraq. The LORD decreed over 2,500 years ago through the prophet Micah that last day Zion would wage war on her enemies in Iraq to gain victory over those who terrorize her. This is Zion's war on terror. It is becoming more apparent that this cannot be the church, the house of Judah, or a millennial event. It is the House of Israel and the time is now. And still, more trouble is brewing on the home front. Her troops are in Iraq fighting a war on terror, and the domestic scene is fraught with upheaval because of the son of perdition fiasco. Gog and Magog are waiting in the wings, and it is the perfect storm.

> *11 - Now also many nations are gathered against thee, that say, Let her be defiled, and let our eye look upon Zion.*

Gog and Magog launch their last day attack on Zion. A surprise coalition comes against her when she least expects it. When does all of this occur? When she is travailing to birth in a king, and when she's waging war on terror in Iraq. And though the situation appears bleak for Zion, there is a silver lining.

> *12 - But they know not the thoughts of the LORD, neither understand they his counsel: for he shall gather them as the sheaves into the floor.*

The nations who attack Zion intend to destroy her, but GOD does not permit it to happen! God merely uses them to cleanse her land of everything that is not Kingdom compatible. By the time we reach this moment, the return of Christ and the Kingdom age is rapidly approaching. God is just getting Zion ready for the fullest manifestation of the Kingdom on earth. His transitional government is being assembled, because a new era is about to begin. The righteous in Zion will weather the storm and emerge from the ark to a new world. God's government awaits! He ultimately leaves the righteous within Zion victorious, and the tares are gathered into bundles and burned. As for Zion? She is no weak-kneed dragon-weakened nation any longer.

> *13 - Arise and thresh, O daughter of Zion: for I will make thine horn iron, and I will make thy hoofs brass: and thou shalt beat in pieces many people: and I will consecrate their gain unto the LORD, and their substance unto the LORD of the whole earth.*

God's purpose for Zion prevails, and Zion is redeemed with judgment. Game, set and match go to Zion, and the glory belongs to God!

So does the story blend? The answer is a resounding "yes".

Coming up in our next chapter of study we will take one final look at a very detailed passage of scripture focusing on Zion's final affliction. This will help you understand the magnitude of *Ezekiel 38*. Following that is our final chapter, and there a grand finale' awaits. It is the family reunion between the House of Israel and the House of Judah. This time it will be under Christ. We are close to the fulfillment of these things, but between now and then Zion has yet to travail.

CHAPTER 9

When Zion Travails

Z ion. The mountain of the LORD. The nation exalted above all others, and people flow to it. So says *Micah 4:1*. In *Psalms 48* David describes Zion as beautiful for situation, the joy of the whole earth, the house of God. The story of America is an incredible story in the scripture, and everything we are is due to God's grace shed upon we the people. I desire to live in no other land.

In this final look at the affliction coming to Zion, we will turn to yet another passage of scripture. Another facet will be chiseled into the body of knowledge that hopefully now is beginning to sparkle in your mind. But first, I want to spend a few moments studying the effects of grasshoppers on agriculture. Yes, you heard me correctly. This may seem unrelated, but you will understand as we study things out. In the process, you will need to ask the critical question. Will it blend? Does it tell the same story? We will find out as we work our way through *Joel 1*. Listen to how the prophet Joel comes on the scene in the House of Israel, and what he reports. Imagine him for a moment standing before the nation as he speaks these words.

Joel 1:

> *1 - The word of the LORD that came to Joel the son of Pethuel.*

> *2 - Hear this, ye old men, and give ear, all ye inhabitants of the land. Hath this been in your days, or even in the days of your fathers?*

Think of the question "*hath this been*". We have to ask the question, what is "*this*"? Whatever "*this*" is must be important because Joel tells the people to do something with it.

3 - Tell ye your children of it, and let your children tell their children, and their children another generation.

He instructs Israel to tell future generations about "*this*" or "*it*". OK Joel, that's great. But we don't know what "*this*" is! And we're supposed to tell our children of "*it*"? At this juncture, we don't know what Joel is referencing. Rest assured, he is about to tell them.

4 - That which the palmerworm hath left hath the locust eaten; and that which the locust hath left hath the cankerworm eaten; and that which the cankerworm hath left hath the caterpiller eaten.

Here we find him now describing the effects of a plague of locusts, cankerworms, and caterpillars. They are devouring everything, and this is the "*this*" that he is talking about. Historically we know the occasion for Joel's lament stems from an invasion of insects that swept the land and ate everything in sight. That may sound like a nuisance for a city dweller, but for an agricultural community that spells utter destruction and it is the undercurrent of a societal collapse. It represents the loss of everything from the Gross Domestic Product to the food on the table. It touches everyone!

5 - Awake, ye drunkards, and weep; and howl, all ye drinkers of wine, because of the new wine; for it is cut off from your mouth.

The work of these insects is so complete, the party crowd can't even feed their vice. There is nothing left of the grapes with which to make a new batch of wine. These insects are destroying everything from the necessities to the pleasantries.

6 - For a nation is come up upon my land, strong, and without number, whose teeth are the teeth of a lion, and he hath the cheek teeth of a great lion.

Here Joel switches labels and refers to this swarm of insects as a nation. In doing so, it denotes union and organization in their endeavors to eat up everything in sight. They are described as strong, without number, and fierce like the king of beasts.

121

7 - He hath laid my vine waste, and barked my fig tree: he hath made it clean bare, and cast it away; the branches thereof are made white.

Everything is devoured by this invading horde of insects! They don't just settle for the fruit on the trees, they even eat away the bark. For the tree, that spells the end of its life. In other words, these insects don't just devour the produce; they also devour the production machine. And just what can Israel do?

8 - Lament like a virgin girded with sackcloth for the husband of her youth.

9 - The meat offering and the drink offering is cut off from the house of the LORD; the priests, the LORD's ministers, mourn.

Their only response is to mourn. Frankly, at this point in time I doubt a stirring message on greed and prosperity is going to dig them out of this hole. There is no amount of positive speaking that will turn the tide and another offering and synagogue building program won't hold any relevance. You cannot eat a beautifully decorated sanctuary, and what these people need is food.

10 - The field is wasted, the land mourneth; for the corn is wasted: the new wine is dried up, the oil languisheth.

11 - Be ye ashamed, O ye husbandmen; howl, O ye vinedressers, for the wheat and for the barley; because the harvest of the field is perished.

12 - The vine is dried up, and the fig tree languisheth; the pomegranate tree, the palm tree also, and the apple tree, even all the trees of the field, are withered: because joy is withered away from the sons of men.

Joel has a tough job here, and it is to present very bad news. There is little to be happy about, and lest you think that crop dusting and insecticide are the solution, read on.

13 - Gird yourselves, and lament, ye priests: howl, ye ministers of the altar: come, lie all night in sackcloth, ye ministers of my God: for the meat offering and the drink offering is withholden from the house of your God.

14 - Sanctify ye a fast, call a solemn assembly, gather the elders and all the inhabitants of the land into the house of the LORD your God, and cry unto the LORD,

The only answer against this invasion is mass repentance! Even by the priests. It is not bigger church buildings and fancier productions needed now. These things are silly in the grand scope of things, and the only thing pleasing to God is a desperate turning to Him. It is a wrecking of the status quo in favor of the entire culture turning back to God. And one can see the total destruction by this army of insects in the last few verses of this passage.

15 - Alas for the day! for the day of the LORD is at hand, and as a destruction from the Almighty shall it come.

Joel now says something of great importance. He correlates this invasion of locusts to "*the day of the LORD*"; something yet to come. It is interesting that he would refer to it as such, and we will find out why in the verses ahead.

16 - Is not the meat cut off before our eyes, yea, joy and gladness from the house of our God?

17 - The seed is rotten under their clods, the garners are laid desolate, the barns are broken down; for the corn is withered.

18 - How do the beasts groan! the herds of cattle are perplexed, because they have no pasture; yea, the flocks of sheep are made desolate.

19 - O LORD, to thee will I cry: for the fire hath devoured the pastures of the wilderness, and the flame hath burned all the trees of the field.

20 - The beasts of the field cry also unto thee: for the rivers of waters are dried up, and the fire hath devoured the pastures of the wilderness.

In short, all of the natural resources used by the people are completely devoured by this invasion. Even the beasts of the field cannot find pasture, and things look pretty bleak. This event is so bad, it was worth retelling, and this is what he tells Israel to tell her future generations about in verses 2-3. And if you did not know before now, this is the effect of grasshoppers on agriculture.

The obvious question however is this: What does this have to do with our study of last day Zion? The answer is found in the next chapter, where the vision expands and Joel is no longer reporting on what has been. In *Joel 2* he reports on what will be, and likens a last day invasion of Zion to look like this invasion of locusts. Consider that his storyline is being directed by the Spirit of God, and Joel is not embellishing it for the listener. It is God using this event to establish a benchmark for what Zion will face in the last days, and then inspiring Joel to tell the story so the final generations in Zion will understand the magnitude of their final battle. If you dare to find out, let us read on and explore *Joel 2*.

Joel 2:

1 - Blow ye the trumpet in Zion, and sound an alarm in my holy mountain: let all the inhabitants of the land tremble: for the day of the LORD cometh, for it is nigh at hand;

Once again, Zion is referred to as God's holy mountain. We know from *Micah* that it is established in the last days, so we can draw the conclusion that what follows in this passage of scripture is a last day event. And if you live in Zion, it is coming soon to a street corner near you. It is described as the day of the LORD, which we know from *Joel 1:15* is a day of destruction. The day of the LORD as applied to Zion is like an invasion of locusts that will devour everything. As we read through *Joel 2* you will see that the passage is:

- A protracted view . . .
- Given by Joel . . .

- Of the invasion that Micah alludes to . . .
- When Zion is embroiled in Iraq . . .
- When Zion is struggling to birth a king . . .
- And her enemies attack her.

It is:

> *2 - A day of darkness and of gloominess, a day of clouds and of thick darkness, as the morning spread upon the mountains: a great people and a strong; there hath not been ever the like, neither shall be any more after it, even to the years of many generations.*

Now we see the invading military force coming against Zion. They are a force described as endless and strong. Just like the insects in *Joel 1*. It is described as the largest military operation the world has ever seen or ever will see. This describes the enemy attacking Zion, and in the coming verse we also see its tactics used against Zion.

> *3 - A fire devoureth before them; and behind them a flame burneth: the land is as the garden of Eden before them, and behind them a desolate wilderness; yea, and nothing shall escape them.*

Simply put, they burn and eat everything in sight. The enemy employs a warfare tactic known as "scorched earth", and both Russia and China are very acquainted with it. It eliminates the resources of the population that may be used to strengthen them or fight back.

It is also indicated here that the invaders are using the abundance of Zion to resupply their own effort. With lengthy supply lines extending back to their own countries, the thugs must forage for their own sustenance. The solution is to eat and devour everything in sight, for the land before them is as the "*garden of Eden*". Behind them, nothing is left. They devour everything they encounter.

These conditions of warfare are banned by the Geneva Convention, but that will not matter. This is a no-holds-barred assault on Zion, and the invaders are determined to prevail. The rules of engagement as outlined by the Geneva Convention are largely put together by the Saxon people, and

Islam and Communism have never played by our rules. When this battle ensues, do not make the fatal mistake of assuming that the invaders are going to play nice and play by our rules.

> *4 - The appearance of them is as the appearance of horses; and as horsemen, so shall they run.*

> *5 - Like the noise of chariots on the tops of mountains shall they leap, like the noise of a flame of fire that devoureth the stubble, as a strong people set in battle array.*

Tanks, helicopters, aircraft and the devices of modern war did not exist in Joel's day. So he's describing the instruments of war in this last day battle as best as he can. He describes the reaction of Zion's citizenry in the next verse.

> *6 - Before their face the people shall be much pained: all faces shall gather blackness.*

The countenance of the people is not one of confidence; it is one of fear and pain. This is not a terrorist attack on a train station; this is an all-out invasion. The people have been dwelling in peace and safety . . . until now. They have not been at war; they have been at the mall. They have been living their best lives now, and this invasion takes them entirely by surprise. They have not heard of this in church; they have only heard things that tickle their ears. They are not conditioned physically, spiritually or mentally for this battle. And now this sleepy civilian population, with no chain of command, with no resident military to protect her, must face the mightiest army in the history of mankind. It is the Dragon vs. the Woman, and the Woman is at a major disadvantage. Here is what Zion will be up against:

> *7 - They shall run like mighty men; they shall climb the wall like men of war; and they shall march every one on his ways, and they shall not break their ranks:*

Zion will face a military machine unrivaled in human history. They will be organized, and they won't use the door. They won't bring a search warrant, they will bring guns. With porous borders, these invaders will pour unhindered into our land in droves.

> *8 - Neither shall one thrust another; they shall walk every one in his path: and when they fall upon the sword, they shall not be wounded.*

It looks as if they will face some limited resistance. Americans own weapons, and this is a good thing. For this period in time, Jesus even instructed us to sell our extra garments and buy a "sword" if we do not have one. A .45 caliber "sword" should be in every closet of the land if we take Jesus' words seriously. But initially any attempts to organize resistance will not faze the enemy. The invaders will not be deterred; they will just keep coming. It begs an interesting question. If attempts to organize a fight to save the land are premature at this point, what can the civilian population do as a right response to this invasion? If organized and direct engagement will not stop them, what are we to do? This will be detailed by scripture in a few moments, but for now there is more to be said about the actions of the invading army. It is a moving, eating, devouring machine.

> *9 - They shall run to and fro in the city; they shall run upon the wall, they shall climb up upon the houses; they shall enter in at the windows like a thief.*

They are pouring over the borders and moving into Zion. As they go they are encountering cities and homes. Places that are occupied, and that have the supplies they need. When they come to the houses, they won't come with a warrant. They will come with a gun. They won't knock and wait for an answer either. They won't even use the doors. They will kick out the windows and come on in. If you are unfortunate enough to be caught in this situation, be prepared to defend your turf. You may die in the process, but death is better than being taken alive by this horde. At best, you may be able to stop them from entering your home, but they will continue to roll inland as they keep coming, and coming, and coming.

On a practical note, bear in mind that you must be prepared to survive the collapse of WalMart. When hell unleashes its fury against Zion, the shelves of your local grocer will be bare within minutes. And a supply truck is not coming to restock them. This form of distribution is over! You would do well to have some supplies because there won't be any around for you to buy. But still, the most important thing to do has yet to be detailed, and we will see what it is shortly.

> *10 - The earth shall quake before them; the heavens shall tremble: the sun and the moon shall be dark, and the stars shall withdraw their shining:*

This could be both literal and symbolic. To Israel, it is going feel like God has abandoned them!

> *11 - And the LORD shall utter his voice before his army: for his camp is very great: for he is strong that executeth his word: for the day of the LORD is great and very terrible; and who can abide it?*

Question: Why would God refer to this as His army?

Answer: It is the tool used to cleanse the land of unrighteousness.

Jesus told us in *Matthew 13* that the wheat and the tares are going to grow together. But at the very end He is going to gather together the tares and burn them. Their last chance is done, and now it's time to remove them from the Kingdom of Heaven. This army of God is moving at God's command, and can only do what He commands. Zion is going to discover a side of God that we are not acquainted with, and that is the fierceness of His wrath when He reaches the boiling point against a sinful people. The obvious conclusion is that you do not want to be in the LORD's crosshairs from today forward! If this army is marching at His command, you need the blood over the doorposts of your home, for that is your only place of safety! And just as with the plague of locusts, the solution is not crop-dusting and insecticide (which in this case would be organized and direct resistance). What God is looking for first from the people is repentance. This is detailed in the following verses.

> *12 - Therefore also now, saith the LORD, turn ye even to me with all your heart, and with fasting, and with weeping, and with mourning:*

13 - And rend your heart, and not your garments, and turn unto the LORD your God: for he is gracious and merciful, slow to anger, and of great kindness, and repenteth him of the evil.

14 - Who knoweth if he will return and repent, and leave a blessing behind him; even a meat offering and a drink offering unto the LORD your God?

God does not want this to be a protracted beating, and the outcome now hangs on the response of the people. He is waiting to see how we will respond, and the prophet is indicating that God WANTS to bring blessing back to the land. But He is waiting for the people. Here then is the commission placed before the people of God in the day when these events unfold:

15 - Blow the trumpet in Zion, sanctify a fast, call a solemn assembly:

16 - Gather the people, sanctify the congregation, assemble the elders, gather the children, and those that suck the breasts: let the bridegroom go forth of his chamber, and the bride out of her closet.

17 - Let the priests, the ministers of the LORD, weep between the porch and the altar, and let them say, Spare thy people, O LORD, and give not thine heritage to reproach, that the heathen should rule over them: wherefore should they say among the people, Where is their God?

It is time for Zion to get back to the basics. They were established as one nation under God, and a national "come to Jesus" meeting is the only appropriate response now. It is not a church service that God is looking for now, He is looking for a whole-hearted return by the people to the laws of God. Before resistance will prosper, repentance must take place. There must be a suspension of business as usual, even by the ministers in the land. A lot could be said about the lethargy of the modern Christian and this invasion brings it to the forefront with great clarity. Business as usual is not cutting it! It is wholly distasteful to God, and desperate times call for desperate measures. This is the call of the prophet to the people when this event takes them by surprise.

Additionally, I see an awakening by the people as to who they are. They suddenly realize that they are God's heritage . . . one nation under God . . . and they are now awake to the obligations associated with that. Consequently they are asking God for unmerited favor and another chance. The cry of the people amounts to this; "God, we see who we are, and how we've messed up. Please forgive us and don't let this wicked people rule over us. WE ARE YOUR NATION!" That will be the foundation for every cry made in the land at this time. Thank God for His mercy, because things are about to take a turn.

> *18 - Then will the LORD be jealous for his land, and pity his people.*

God is faithful, even though we the people have not been faithful. And as seen here, God has a land! And a people! It is the House of Israel in its land in the uttermost part of the earth. It is US; it is "Ammarica"; the Kingdom of Heaven on earth. The good news is that from here forward, the Woman is kept in safety in the wilderness. This is the moment I want to live to see.

> *19 - Yea, the LORD will answer and say unto his people, Behold, I will send you corn, and wine, and oil, and ye shall be satisfied therewith: and I will no more make you a reproach among the heathen:*

> *20 - But I will remove far off from you the northern army, and will drive him into a land barren and desolate, with his face toward the east sea, and his hinder part toward the utmost sea, and his stink shall come up, and his ill savour shall come up, because he hath done great things.*

The northern army is that of Gog and Magog, and they have accomplished God's purpose of cleansing the land of evil. Based on where he is facing (the east sea or the Atlantic Ocean), and what his backside is facing (the utmost sea or Pacific Ocean), it looks as if his invasion route has been from the West Coast inward towards the heartland. And now it is time for God to destroy Gog and Magog. The tide is about to turn, and it's going to be a bloodbath. This alliance that has attacked God's land will not be spared, and the body count is going to create quite a stink in the land. *Ezekiel 39:11* says it will "*stop the noses*" of people traveling close by. He is going to draw Gog into a kill box, and destroy them ALL. When the repentance is complete, the time comes to take up arms and fight. This victory will begin with repentance, but it will end with bullets. *Ezekiel 38:21* says that God will "*call for a sword against him*", and this is the call to stand and fight. America is still worth fighting for, and you must be prepared to stand in her defense in the days ahead.

This is purely speculation, but based on *Joel 2:20* it almost sounds like the invaders are pushed into Wyoming. Why would I say Wyoming? First of all, it is a barren and desolate land in proximity to THE mountain range of the nation . . . the Rocky Mountains. Where ever Gog and Magog are stopped must be both a barren and desolate place, as well as a mountainous place according to *Ezekiel 38:12*. It reads "*And I will call for a sword against him throughout all my mountains, saith the LORD GOD: every man's sword shall be against his brother*. Wyoming satisfies both criteria. Additionally, *Ezekiel 38:22* says "*And I will plead against him with pestilence and with blood; and I will rain upon him, and upon his bands, and upon the many people that are with him, an overflowing rain, and great hailstones, fire, and brimstone*." This is how God shows the nation that HE is the one responsible for their victory. The people are fighting, but it is almost as if God is showing off a little. He is God, and He's allowed to do that. There is no better way to prove to the people that they are one nation under one God! *Ezekiel 38:23* says "*Thus will I magnify myself, and sanctify myself; and I will be known in the eyes of many nations, and they shall know that I am the LORD*." So victory comes to the people as they fight, and God fights alongside of them. In the barren / mountainous place of victory, it also must be a location that has the ingredients capable of producing torrential rain, hail, fire and brimstone. Central Wyoming to Southern Colorado is the hail capital of the world. Could it be that the thugs are pushed into this barren and desolate land next to the Rockies, only to get hammered with the great hail this region is known for? And to top off the whole thing, Yellowstone could erupt. This would produce a volcanic event that rains fire and brimstone upon them as well. We do not know for sure, but it is food for thought. Rest assured it will happen somewhere in this nation, and the place of victory will have a name. In the meantime, don't contract a case of NIMBY (not in my back yard) disease. The American Christian has been conditioned to accept the fulfillment of scripture as being entirely overseas. Somehow we have come to believe that we get to watch it all in High Definition on our flat screen TV's. We accept the names of specific locations; places like the Red Sea, the Mount of Olives, Jerusalem, etc.. We are OK with those names as long as they are not in my back yard. But if Zion is the United States, the mountainous region described above is not in proximity to the Mount of Olives. The name tag will be American, and it could be the Ozarks, the Black Hills, the Cascades, or the Rockies. Joel described it as he saw it in his vision, but it will have the name of a state, mountain range, county, city, and even a zip code. It may be in your back yard, so read and re-read these passages to understand what the prophets are seeing. Maybe you too will see with the eyes of your spirit and understand the specifics as we move into the time of fulfillment. Continuing onward now with *Joel 2*, good news awaits:

> *21 - Fear not, O land; be glad and rejoice: for the LORD will do great things.*

> *22 - Be not afraid, ye beasts of the field: for the pastures of the wilderness do spring, for the tree beareth her fruit, the fig tree and the vine do yield their strength.*

Quite literally, it sounds like deliverance comes in the spring time of the year. I do not see this as a protracted event. It could extend from the season of birth for the Manchild (an election season in late fall) to sometime in the spring. The bulk of it would occur over a winter period, and this is the time of winter flight to the wilderness that Jesus alludes to in *Matthew 24:20*. They are the same story!

> *23 - Be glad then, ye children of Zion, and rejoice in the LORD your God: for he hath given you the former rain moderately, and he will cause to come down for you the rain, the former rain, and the latter rain in the first month.*

> *24 - And the floors shall be full of wheat, and the vats shall overflow with wine and oil.*

> *25 - And I will restore to you the years that the locust hath eaten, the cankerworm, and the caterpiller, and the palmerworm, my great army which I sent among you.*

> *26 - And ye shall eat in plenty, and be satisfied, and praise the name of the LORD your God, that hath dealt wondrously with you: and my people shall never be ashamed.*

Blessing returns to the people of Zion! They exist in a protected state from this time forward! The Temple has been cleansed! And do you remember the words found in *Ezekiel 39:7*? It reads "*So will I make my holy name known in the midst of my people Israel; and I will not let them pollute my Holy Name any more*". This is Israel's final battle, and she will never be corrupted or afflicted again.

> *27 - And ye shall know that I am in the midst of Israel, and that I am the LORD your God, and none else: and my people shall never be ashamed.*

And finally, here is definite proof that the House of Israel is Zion. This verse ends any speculation to that end. The eyes of the House of Israel are now open to their heritage and associated obligations, and after all this has happened, it is celebration time.

> *28 - And it shall come to pass afterward, that I will pour out my spirit upon all flesh; and your sons and your daughters shall prophesy, your old men shall dream dreams, your young men shall see visions:*

> *29 - And also upon the servants and upon the handmaids in those days will I pour out my spirit.*

> *30 - And I will shew wonders in the heavens and in the earth, blood, and fire, and pillars of smoke.*

> *31 - The sun shall be turned into darkness, and the moon into blood, before the great and terrible day of the LORD come.*

> *32 - And it shall come to pass, that whosoever shall call on the name of the LORD shall be delivered: for in mount Zion and in Jerusalem shall be deliverance, as the LORD hath said, and in the remnant whom the LORD shall call.*

Ezekiel also makes this observation in very succinct terms. *Ezekiel 39:29* says *"Neither will I hide my face any more from them: for I have poured out my spirit upon the house of Israel, saith the LORD GOD"*. The renewal has begun.

Several years ago I came across an article that is worth sharing. Snopes has rendered it as inauthentic, but people "in the know" know that Snopes is a left-leaning group that has invalidated a lot of truth consistent with its agenda to revise American history. The article I share has a simple title. It is called George Washington's Vision, and it provides detail of a vision by America's first Commander in Chief. I present it now, with a few of my thoughts interspersed throughout.

George Washington's Vision:

The father of our country, George Washington, was a man of prayer. Many of us have read of how he went to the thicket many times to pray during the winter his army was at Valley Forge. However, little publicity has been given to the vision and prophecy he received at that time.

The account of this vision was given in 1859 by an old soldier. He gave it to a writer, Wesley Bradshaw, who published it. In the vision God revealed to George Washington that three great perils would come upon the republic. He was given to know that America was going through the first peril at that time. The old soldier who told the story of the vision said the nation would soon see the account verified by the second peril descending upon the land.

We give the account here as printed in the U.S. war veterans paper The National Tribune, in December 1880. The National Tribune became "The Stars and Stripes", and this article was later reprinted in that publication. Here are the words of Washington as stated by this old soldier:

I do not know whether it is owing to the anxiety of my mind, or what, but this afternoon, as I was sitting at this table engaging in preparing a dispatch, something in the apartment seemed to disturb me. Looking up, I beheld standing opposite to me a singularly beautiful being. So astonished was I, for I had given strict orders not to be disturbed that it was some moments before I found language to inquire the cause of the visit. A second, a third, and even a fourth time did I repeat my question, but received no answer from my mysterious visitor except a slight raising of the eyes.

By this time I felt strange sensations spreading through me. I would have risen but the riveted gaze of the being before me rendered volition impossible. I tried once more to speak, but my tongue became useless, as if paralyzed. A new influence, mysterious, potent, irresistible, took possession of me. All I could do was to gaze steadily, vacantly at my unknown visitor.

Gradually the surrounding atmosphere seemed to fill with sensations, and grew luminous. Everything about me seemed to rarefy, the mysterious visitor also becoming more airy and yet more distinct to my sight than before. I began to feel as one dying, or rather to experience the sensations I sometimes imagine accompanying death. I did not think, I did not reason, I did not move. All were alike impossible. I was only conscious of gazing fixedly, vacantly on my companion.

Presently I heard a voice say, "Son of the Republic, look and learn," while at the same time my visitor extended an arm eastward.

I now beheld a heavy white vapor at some distance rising fold upon fold. This gradually dissipated, and I looked upon the strange scene. Before me lay, out in one vast plain all the countries of the world—Europe, Asia, Africa, and America. I saw rolling and tossing between Europe and America lay billows of the Atlantic, and between Asia and America lay the Pacific.

"Son of the Republic", said the same mysterious voice as before, "Look and learn."

At that moment I beheld a dark shadowy being, like an angel, standing, or rather floating in mid-air, between Europe and America. Dipping water out of the ocean in the hollow of each hand, he sprinkled some upon America with his right hand, while with his left he cast some over Europe. Immediately a cloud arose from these countries and joined in mid-ocean. For awhile it remained stationary, and then it moved slowly westward, until it enveloped America in its murky folds. Sharp flashs of lightning gleamed through at intervals, and I heard the smothered groans and cries of the American People.

My note: This could be interpreted as the Revolutionary War then in progress.

A second time the angel dipped water from the ocean and sprinkled it out as before. The dark cloud drew back to the ocean, in whose heaving billows it sank from view.

A third time I heard the mysterious voice saying, "Son of the Republic, look and learn."

I cast my eyes upon America and beheld villages and town and cities spring up one right after another until the whole land from the Atlantic to the Pacific was dotted with them. Again, I heard the mysterious voice say,

"Son of the Republic, the end of the century cometh, look and learn."

And this time a dark shadowy angel turned his face southward. From Africa I saw an ill omened specter approach our land. It flitted slowly and heavily over every town and city of the latter. The inhabitants presently set themselves in battle array against each other. As I continued looking I saw a bright angel on whose brow was traced the word 'Union.' He was bearing the American flag. He placed the flag between the divided nation and said, "Remember, ye are brethren."

My note: A future look at the Civil War? I believe so.

Instantly the inhabitants, casting down their weapons became friends once more, and united around the National Standard.

Again I heard a mysterious voice saying, "Son of the Republic, look and learn."

At this the dark, shadowy angel placed a trumpet to his mouth, and blew three distinct blasts; and taking water from the ocean, he sprinkled it upon Europe, Asia, and Africa.

My note: Three blasts signifying WWIII? The conflict of *Ezekiel 38* & *Joel 2*? The continents mentioned line up with the alliance of nations in *Ezekiel 38*. Measure it against the Word of God and come to your own conclusions.

Then my eyes beheld a fearful scene. From each of these continents arose thick black clouds that were soon joined into one. And throughout this mass there gleamed a dark red light by which I saw hordes of armed men. These men, moving with the cloud marched by land and sailed by sea to America, which country was enveloped in the volume of the cloud. And I dimly saw these vast armies devastate the whole country and burn the villages, towns and cities, which I had seen spring up.

As my ears listened to the thundering of the cannon, clashing of swords, and the shouts and cries of millions in mortal combat, I again heard the mysterious voice saying, "Son of the Republic, look and learn."

When the voice had ceased, the dark shadowy angel placed his trumpet once more to his mouth, and blew a long and fearful blast. Instantly a light, as of a thousand suns shone down from above me, and pierced and broke into fragments of the dark cloud, which enveloped America. At the same moment the angel upon whose head still shown the word 'Union,' and who bore our national flag in one hand and a sword in the other, descended from the heavens attended by legions of white spirits. These immediately joined the inhabitants of America, who I perceived were well-nigh over come, but who immediately taking courage again, closed up their broken ranks, and renewed battle.

Again amid the fearful voice of the conflict I heard the mysterious voice say, "Son of the Republic, look and learn."

As the voice ceased, the shadowy angel for the last time dipped the water from the ocean and sprinkled it upon America. Instantly the dark clouds rolled back, together with the armies it had brought, leaving the inhabitants of the land victorious.

Then once more I beheld the villages, towns and cities springing up where I had seen them before, while the bright angel, planting the azure standard cried with a loud voice: "While the stars remain, and the heavens send down dew upon the earth, so long shall the Union last." And taking from his brow the crown, which blazoned the word 'Union,' he placed it down upon the standard while the people, kneeling down said, 'Amen.'

The scene instantly began to fade and dissolve, and I at last saw nothing but the rising, curling vapor, I at first beheld. This also disappeared, and I found myself once more gazing upon the mysterious visitor who, in the same voice I heard before said, "Son of the Republic, what you have seen is thus interpreted: Three great perils will come upon the Republic. The most fearful for her is the third. But the whole world united shall not prevail against her. Let every child of the Republic learn to live for his God, his land and Union." With these words the vision vanished, and I started from my seat and felt that I had seen a vision wherein had been showed me the birth, progress, and destiny of the United States."

I present this vision because there are many parallels to scriptures we have studied in this book. Notice the countries involved. Note the ferocity of the final conflict. See the hopelessness of the nation's condition. Rejoice in the intervention by God. It is all over be it not for the hand of GOD on behalf of His land and His people. God glorifies HIMSELF through giving us the victory. Does it blend? Yes it does.

In closing, I want to provide some reassurance to the reader of God's loving kindness. We began with *Ezekiel 38* and the coming war, and we find ourselves back where we started. To a nation that views wealth and ease as entitlements, I know this generates a myriad of emotions. Perhaps even denial. But I want to point you back to God's agenda through all of this, and it is found for Zion in the book of *Isaiah*.

Isaiah 1:

> *25 - I will turn my hand upon thee, and purely purge away thy dross, and take away all thy tin:*

> *26 - And I will restore thy judges as at the first, and thy counsellors as at the beginning: afterward thou shalt be called, The city of righteousness, the faithful city.*

27 - Zion shall be redeemed with judgment, and her converts with righteousness.

28 - And the destruction of the transgressors and of the sinners shall be together, and they that forsake the LORD shall be consumed.

Zion shall be redeemed with judgment! In other words, this is what saves her! Though unpleasant to read about, and even more unpleasant to observe, the coming upheaval will liberate God-fearing patriots to serve Him the way we should. Everything will be set aright in America the way it should be. So the bad news is also the good news. This is not God moving against us to destroy us, it is the hand of God being used to cleanse and deliver us.

For the House of Israel, this marks the end of her conflict. For the House of Judah, it is just beginning as detailed in *Joel 3*. You may want to read that passage of scripture on your own, and see what the Lord reveals to you. You are a wiser student now than when you started this book. Since we have focused in large degree on the House of Israel, our study of the war doctrine is now concluded. Once the House of Judah is ready, a family reunion awaits. A family reunion between the House of Israel and the House of Judah! This is the grand finale and something God has been working towards for literally thousands of years. This is a day I hope to live to see, and we will close out our study with this subject next.

CHAPTER 10

The Family Reunion

This chapter is the 10th and "final" part of our study, and this will bring a degree of closure to the subject. Closure does not mean it is the end of the study; it just means we've covered the topic sufficiently to lay the right foundation. Hopefully you have acquired a reasonable knowledge base from which you can better understand the prophetic Word and measure the world situation with it. With the knowledge you now have, I would challenge you to reread the entire Bible and see what the LORD reveals to you on your own. There is always speculation involved when we look forward, but with the right foundation it can be an informed speculation that hits close to the mark. A bull's eye may even be possible as God reveals His plan and we rightly divide the Word of Truth. As time marches on towards the final conflict, perhaps the LORD will reveal to you some needed information necessary for the defense of our nation.

These events we have studied obviously create global upheaval and a change in our two primary national players: the House of Israel and the House of Judah. Once the upheaval has ended for both nations, how will this era conclude nationally for these two nations? To help us find the answer, we will visit two Biblical passages that provide the clarity we need. Our first stop will be in *Hosea 1*. As has been my custom, the Word will be presented in addition to necessary commentary. The grand finale awaits.

Hosea 1:

> *1 - The word of the LORD that came unto Hosea, the son of Beeri, in the days of Uzziah, Jotham, Ahaz, and Hezekiah, kings of Judah, and in the days of Jeroboam the son of Joash, king of Israel.*

> *2 - The beginning of the word of the LORD by Hosea. And the LORD said to Hosea, Go, take unto thee a wife of whoredoms and children of whoredoms: for the land hath committed great whoredom, departing from the LORD.*

Lest you desire to be a prophet, understand that God often gave them some strange assignments. Here we see that God intends to use Hosea's domestic life as an illustrated example of Israel's relationship to God. Israel was chosen by God to be His bride, but she has chosen to be unfaithful, a whore. She has gone after strange gods and lovers, and God wants Hosea to model that and all the associated heartache before the eyes of the people. It is not a fun job, but it is necessary to illustrate to the House of Israel their sin in living color. God is about to show the House of Israel their future through the domestic life of His prophet Hosea. Here is what Hosea does at God's command:

> *3 - So he went and took Gomer the daughter of Diblaim; which conceived, and bare him a son.*

> *4 - And the LORD said unto him, Call his name Jezreel; for yet a little while, and I will avenge the blood of Jezreel upon the house of Jehu, and will cause to cease the kingdom of the house of Israel.*

> *5 - And it shall come to pass at that day, that I will break the bow of Israel, in the valley of Jezreel.*

This is not so much about the birth of a child as it is what God wants this child to represent to the House of Israel. God names the child Jezreel, likening him to the end of Jehu's reign as King over the House of Israel. You can read about the account on your own in *2 Kings*. Suffice it to say that Jezreel's existence as Hosea's firstborn is connected to the dissolving of the House of Israel as a kingdom. For our study, we just need to remember the name, his birth order, and event which it signifies. Jezreel symbolizes the House of Israel's captivity by the Assyrians and the subsequent fall of their kingdom. It is the first of three major events to occur to the House of Israel, and the second event is foretold through the birth of yet another child to Hosea:

> *6 - And she conceived again, and bare a daughter. And God said unto him, Call her name Loruhamah: for I will no more have mercy upon the house of Israel; but I will utterly take them away.*

This child represents the second event to occur with the House of Israel after their time in captivity at the hand of the Assyrians had ended. This foretells that the House of Israel will be scattered, never to return to their original homeland in Palestine. As we know from chapter 1 of this study, Judah did remain in the regions of Palestine as seen in the next verse.

> *7 - But I will have mercy upon the house of Judah, and will save them by the LORD their God, and will not save them by bow, nor by sword, nor by battle, by horses, nor by horsemen.*

Consistent with God's promise, the House of Judah remained behind as Israel scattered, and though a small nation from that point forward God has been their saving grace. For Hosea's storyline, the existence of these two children with prophetic names now detail for the House of Israel two of the three major transitions they will experience. The third phase is foretold next.

> *8 - Now when she had weaned Loruhamah, she conceived, and bare a son.*

> *9 - Then said God, Call his name Loammi: for ye are not my people, and I will not be your God.*

This third child represents the "forgetting" that takes place by the House of Israel as they migrate northward. They forget who they are, and they forget their God. It will occur later on the timeline, after they have scattered and they are migrating towards the uttermost part. This is when they will lose their identity and no longer remember God or their heritage. Yet in spite of their forgetting, the House of Israel is still alive and well. And they are growing larger by the day. This is foretold in the next verse.

> *10a—Yet the number of the children of Israel shall be as the sand of the sea, which cannot be measured nor numbered;*

Though now lost to their heritage, they will be a large people group, a large people group without a clue as to who they are. Obviously this will take place over a large period of time. The things described here do not happen overnight. But in spite of these transitions in the nation, God does not intend to leave the House of Israel in a perpetual state of ignorance as to who they are. There is another transformation that will take place in the House of Israel at some point of time after these three major evolutions have occurred. This one is quite positive. It is found in the latter part of *verse 10*.

> *10b—and it shall come to pass, that in the place where it was said unto them, Ye are not my people, there it shall be said unto them, Ye are the sons of the living God.*

In their latter days, they will not be known as Israel any more. It will even be told to them in their final resting place that they are not Israel. If you tried to tell them they were Israel, they wouldn't believe you because they have taken on a new name. So if they are literally being told that they are not Israel, and even believe they are not Israel, how will they be known? Hosea says they will be called the sons of the living God. If we want the right definition for that phrase, *John 1:12* provides it with great clarity. It says "*that as many as received him, to them gave he power to become the sons of God, even to them that believe on his name*". The sons of the living God as defined by John are people who receive Christ. If the House of Israel will be known as the sons of the living God nationally speaking, it tells me that as a nation they are going to be built on the precepts of Christ. Hosea decrees that the House of Israel will receive the message of Christ and be known as a Christian nation it the latter days. There is only one place today that is a Saxon ('saac's sons) nation identifying with Christianity, and that is the United States. The sons of Isaac have conglomerated in the uttermost part of the earth, and built their nation on Christ. We are living *Hosea 1:10*.

Unfortunately, in spite of this positive turn in the House of Israel in the last days, the united kingdom of Israel remains divided. That is, until we get to our next verse where we read of the final step yet to come for this divided family.

11 - Then shall the children of Judah and the children of Israel be gathered together, and appoint themselves one head, and they shall come up out of the land: for great shall be the day of Jezreel.

Hosea foretells of a future time when the House of Israel (as a Christian nation) and the House of Judah will reunify under one head. The scattering of Jezreel is so "*great*" and far reaching in its effect that the division between the brother nations will remain right up until the time of the very end. The overview of *Hosea 1* spans over 2,000 years. With that as an overview, let's recap the key ingredients and encapsulate it into a shorter version.

- Hosea's focus is on the House of Israel portion of the Kingdom . . .
- Their Kingdom will end and they will be scattered . . .
- As they scatter, they will lose a sense of their identity and take on a different name . . .
- Their new name will be as a Christian nation . . .
- They will join once again with the House of Judah at the end of the age . . .
- And the United Kingdom of Israel will finally have one King.

It is unknown who that King will be at this juncture, but logically speaking, if they are a purified Christian people, their "*one head*" will not be a liberal secularist. The House of Israel is already known as a Christian nation, and they won't want any other king than King Jesus. At this future time, they are completely done with progressivism and the system that enabled the son of perdition, and they are completely unified around one King. Since this is the imagery that God portrays through Hosea's domestic life, imagine for a moment how Hosea would introduce himself and his family to an Israelite. The introduction may sound something like this:

"Hi! My name is Hosea. I represent God. And this is my wife Gomer. She represents Israel, and she is a whore. She should love me and be faithful to me, but she is not. My firstborn is named 'the kingdom will be destroyed'. My second born is named 'Israel will be scattered'. My third born has a longer name. He is named 'Israel will lose her identity . . . be known as the sons of God . . . and Israel and Judah will reunite'. Would you like to come to dinner?" Or something to that effect ☺. That would be quite an introduction, and it would leave the Israelite standing there with their mouth open. That is when Hosea could tell them that his family is a living symbol of the House of Israel's relationship with her God, and a glimpse of what her history will look like extending several millennia into the future. Essentially, *Hosea 1* draws out a continuum of time and events for the House of Israel as it relates to their future days. From *Hosea 2* through *Hosea 14*, he details the many events that the House of Israel will face in this march across time. His writings focus on the House of Israel, and very specifically on Ephraim as the head of that kingdom. He begins with a near-term perspective and ends speaking of her last days. You may want to read it and see what you discover.

The Bible tells us that in the mouth of two or three witnesses everything is established. It is not coincidence that what we have just read in *Hosea* are the same ingredients found in *Ezekiel 37:15-17, 20-28*. There, however, we get a glimpse of who the unified kingdom's one King will be. Let's read it to find out.

Ezekiel 37:

>   *1 - The hand of the LORD was upon me, and carried me out in the spirit of the LORD, and set me down in the midst of the valley which was full of bones,*

>   *2 - And caused me to pass by them round about: and, behold, there were very many in the open valley; and, lo, they were very dry.*

>   *3 - And he said unto me, Son of man, can these bones live? And I answered, O LORD GOD, thou knowest.*

>   *4 - Again he said unto me, Prophesy upon these bones, and say unto them, O ye dry bones, hear the word of the LORD.*

>   *5 - Thus saith the LORD GOD unto these bones; Behold, I will cause breath to enter into you, and ye shall live:*

6 - And I will lay sinews upon you, and will bring up flesh upon you, and cover you with skin, and put breath in you, and ye shall live; and ye shall know that I am the LORD.

7 - So I prophesied as I was commanded: and as I prophesied, there was a noise, and behold a shaking, and the bones came together, bone to his bone.

8 - And when I beheld, lo, the sinews and the flesh came up upon them, and the skin covered them above: but there was no breath in them.

9 - Then said he unto me, Prophesy unto the wind, prophesy, son of man, and say to the wind, Thus saith the Lord GOD; Come from the four winds, O breath, and breathe upon these slain, that they may live.

10 - So I prophesied as he commanded me, and the breath came into them, and they lived, and stood up upon their feet, an exceeding great army.

Rest assured, what we are reading about is not a literal skeleton. The skeleton is a symbol of something larger, and we are about to find out what it is.

11 - Then he said unto me, Son of man, these bones are the whole house of Israel: behold, they say, Our bones are dried, and our hope is lost: we are cut off for our parts.

In our course of study we have learned about the events to come upon both houses of Israel. At what point will all look lost to the whole house of Israel? The answer is pretty simple. It is after the events of the final 3½ years. The House of Israel has dealt with the son of perdition, an insurrection, having no King, and the assault of the dragon. Thankfully this is on the front edge of that period, and that is her final battle. Meanwhile, the House of Judah is dealing with gentile nations trampling down Jerusalem for 3½ years before they are finally in a state of obedience to God. Each nation has gone through the ringer, with slightly different events and for different durations of time. Regardless of the specifics of who faced what, it has been a wearing time for both people groups, and they are still divided as a Kingdom. But what man considers as the end, God often considers as a new beginning. He is not done with them yet!

12 - Therefore prophesy and say unto them, Thus saith the LORD GOD; Behold, O my people, I will open your graves, and cause you to come up out of your graves, and bring you into the land of Israel.

Someone may wonder at this point what Israel's land is. The assumption by many is that this refers only to Palestine. But remember that God has promised much more to them than that, and Israel's land consists of everything in God's promise. It includes everything from Palestine to the uttermost parts of the earth that God gave to Ephraim and Manasseh. When this passage of scripture is ready to be fulfilled, God is telling Israel that it is time for them to FULLY possess EVERYTHING God has promised them.

13 - And ye shall know that I am the LORD, when I have opened your graves, O my people, and brought you up out of your graves,

It also sounds like it is resurrection time. This would place the events of this passage at the end of the 3½ years, just prior to Christ's return. The timing of this will be discussed more a few verses down the page.

14 - And shall put my spirit in you, and ye shall live, and I shall place you in your own land: then shall ye know that I the LORD have spoken it, and performed it, saith the LORD.

These verses are the overview of what both houses will experience at the very end. But now God zooms in to provide a little more detail.

15 - The word of the LORD came again unto me, saying,

16 - Moreover, thou son of man, take thee one stick, and write upon it, For Judah, and for the children of Israel his companions: then take another stick, and write upon it, For Joseph, the stick of Ephraim and for all the house of Israel his companions:

First of all, notice that there are two sticks representing two kingdoms. These are not two doctrines coming together; these are two nations coming together. Hosea was certainly correct when he said the scattering represented by Jezreel, his firstborn, would be far reaching. The greater kingdom of Israel exists in a divided state right up until the very end of time. Each nation is sovereign, and each one has a "stick". If you want to visualize these two sticks, they may look something like this:

What is to become of these two sticks is shown in the following verse.

> *17 - And join them one to another into one stick; and they shall become one in thine hand.*

This is a picture of the coming union between the two houses once again. Hosea decreed it, and now Ezekiel is telling the same story.

> *18 - And when the children of thy people shall speak unto thee, saying, Wilt thou not shew us what thou meanest by these?*

> *19 - Say unto them, Thus saith the LORD GOD; Behold, I will take the stick of Joseph, which is in the hand of Ephraim, and the tribes of Israel his fellows, and will put them with him, even with the stick of Judah, and make them one stick, and they shall be one in mine hand.*

These two distinct national entities have survived apart for thousands of years. But they are now completely joined into one! From a political perspective, this movement is already beginning in the politics of both nations. The people of both Judah and Israel realize that we need to be a united front, but it has not yet been formalized. For it to come to its fullest fruition, imagine the political upheaval that must occur before this will be fully embraced. Even now, the system of the son of perdition and the Beast seek to block the union between the United States and the Jewish state of Israel. Even now, they seek to bring division between the two nations. But most Christian patriots intuitively know in their spirits that America needs to stand with Israel. This is not merely a political position, it is a spiritual one, and God is preparing both houses for a family reunion.

> *20 - And the sticks whereon thou writest shall be in thine hand before their eyes.*

> *21 - And say unto them, Thus saith the LORD GOD; Behold, I will take the children of Israel from among the heathen, whither they be gone, and will gather them on every side, and bring them into their own land:*

> *22 - And I will make them one nation in the land upon the mountains of Israel; and one king shall be king to them all: and they shall be no more two nations, neither shall they be divided into two kingdoms any more at all.*

The location of this union serves as a stumbling block to many, but the seat of power is clearly seen to be in Israel, not in Judah. *Micah 4:7* also confirms it to be Zion. You may want to revisit that scripture to see what it says. Both nations bring something to the table as will be seen shortly in the verses to come.

> *23 - Neither shall they defile themselves any more with their idols, nor with their detestable things, nor with any of their transgressions: but I will save them out of all their dwellingplaces, wherein they have sinned, and will cleanse them: so shall they be my people, and I will be their God.*

We can easily see that this has not happened yet! It will not happen until both nations are wholly turned to Christ. And just who will their King be?

> *24 - And David my servant shall be king over them; and they all shall have one shepherd: they shall also walk in my judgments, and observe my statutes, and do them.*

Ezekiel is not talking about literal David in a resurrected state. He is talking about the Lion of the tribe of Judah . . . the King of Kings . . . prophesied to come from David's lineage. We know Him to be the LORD Jesus Christ! So while ISRAEL produces the GOVERNMENT . . . JUDAH produces the GOVERNOR! These are their respective contributions to a United Kingdom of Israel. For them, it will be no king but King Jesus!

> *25 - And they shall dwell in the land that I have given unto Jacob my servant, wherein your fathers have dwelt; and they shall dwell therein, even they, and their children, and their children's children for ever: and my servant David shall be their prince for ever.*

The time of affliction is over, and globalism is dead! There is no more affinity with wicked ways. There is no more turning to other gods. There is no affinity for any forms of leadership other than that given by God. And now, it is Millennium time!

> *26 - Moreover I will make a covenant of peace with them; it shall be an everlasting covenant with them: and I will place them, and multiply them, and will set my sanctuary in the midst of them for evermore.*

> *27 - My tabernacle also shall be with them: yea, I will be their God, and they shall be my people.*

> *28 - And the heathen shall know that I the LORD do sanctify Israel, when my sanctuary shall be in the midst of them for evermore.*

Jesus said it best on Calvary: It is finished!

God intends to reunify the two nations as one nation under God. In Jesus' own words *"a house divided cannot stand"*. Jesus was not just talking about your domestic life when He made that statement. When He said "*a house divided*", I am certain the disciples knew without a doubt that His primary reference was the divided houses of Israel and Judah. These were Jews who understood their history. The division had been a point of quarrel between them for hundreds of years, and Jesus was declaring a coming reunification. For clarity, I must point out that these two nations did not reunify formally and fulfill *Ezekiel 37* with the establishment of the Jewish State in 1948. Many people think so because this chapter precedes *Ezekiel 38*. But the books of the prophets are not written in chronological order. They often follow a "headline—detail" format of reporting. First they provide the headlines, and then they circle back around and fill in the details. Based on the criteria in *Ezekiel 37*, this cannot happen until the very end of the age after both nations have been cleansed and completely accept the Lordship of Jesus Christ over their national affairs. *Ezekiel 37* actually coincides chronologically with the events of *Ezekiel 47* and takes place just prior to the return of Christ. Understanding these passages also helps to shed new light on New Testament scripture. Consider this passage from *John*:

John 11:47-52

> *47 - Then gathered the chief priests and the Pharisees a council, and said, What do we? for this man doeth many miracles.*

> *48 - If we let him thus alone, all men will believe on him: and the Romans shall come and take away both our place and nation.*

> *49 - And one of them, named Caiaphas, being the high priest that same year, said unto them, Ye know nothing at all,*

> *50 - Nor consider that it is expedient for us, that one man should die for the people, and that the whole nation perish not.*

> *51 - And this spake he not of himself: but being high priest that year, he prophesied that Jesus should die for that nation;*

This verse prompts an immediate question. Who is "*that nation*" a reference to in this verse? Since this was taking place in Judah, and the House of

Judah had maintained its adherence to the laws of Moses, it is easy to conclude that it is the House of Judah. But there's more:

52 - And not for that nation only, but that also he should gather together in one the children of God that were scattered abroad.

Who are "*the children of God scattered abroad*" as referenced in this verse? It cannot be referring to people of faith who would exist around the world in days to come. This is referring to a people that were scattered abroad at that time, and the church as seen in the book of Acts didn't exist yet. This is referring to the House of Israel, and it is talking about a coming reunion between the House of Israel . . . the sons of Isaac . . . Isaac's sons . . . 'saac's sons . . . Saxons . . . and the House of Judah . . . the Jews. They will gather together under Christ!

Saxons and Jews as one nation under God. John is not writing of joining two belief systems here, he is writing of joining two nations under one belief system. Their common faith will be Christianity, and their one King will be King Jesus. Christ will be the framework upon which the two houses will be rejoined. This also helps us conclude that the reunion of *Ezekiel 37* did not happen in 1948. The House of Judah has not yet accepted Jesus as the Messiah, and the House of Israel is increasingly tossing Him aside as well. God's ultimate purpose for Israel is for it to be:

- The Jewish nation . . .
- Plus the conglomerated Saxon nations . . .
- Joined together as one nation under One God . . .
- With one King . . .
- Jesus Christ.

It goes without saying that a lot of house cleaning will occur to make them ready for that. Imagine the political upheaval that must occur to condition both nations for this event. Imagine the impact to global politics through a unified Christ-centered American/Israeli alliance! To Islam / Communism / the UN / and the son of perdition, this is "Zionism" on steroids and is completely intolerable! If they smell it coming, they will take drastic steps to thwart it. Their opposition to this idea is what moves THEM, but they forget that God's favoring of this idea is what moves HIM. And at a future point in time, it will be the driving force behind the political steps taken by both the American and the Jewish State. This is God's idea and it will happen! May we learn to love what God loves, and hate what God hates. Woe to those who call good evil and evil good!

I want to conclude by focusing on one scripture that we read in *Ezekiel*:

Ezekiel 37:

> *19 - Say unto them, Thus saith the LORD GOD; Behold, I will take the stick of Joseph, which is in the hand of Ephraim, and the tribes of Israel his fellows, and will put them with him, even with the stick of Judah, and make them one stick, and they shall be one in mine hand.*

Consider for a moment the importance of these sticks. They obviously serve as symbols for each nation, and we have visualized them as two national flags. Each has distinct symbolism, and each symbol tells a story. Take for instance the symbolism and evolution of the American flag. It did not begin as 13 stripes and 50 stars, and at various points in our history the symbolism spoke of the revolution then taking place. From "Don't Tread On Me" to "Appeal To Heaven", standards have been raised to tell the story of the hour and define the battle lines. These standards were raised to rally American patriots to Heaven's cause. As shown in *Ezekiel 37:19*, every revolution has its symbol, and when the enemy comes in like a flood, the Spirit of the Lord raises up a standard against him.

As stated in the Forward, when America's forefathers signed the Mayflower Compact in 1620, it read in part: *"In the name of God, Amen. We whose names are underwritten . . . having undertaken for the glory of God, and advancement of the Christian faith . . . a voyage to plant the first colony"*. Conceived as one nation under one God, this became the Union standard. During the Revolutionary War, the cry of freedom was "No king but King Jesus". Birthed as one nation under one God, this remained the Union standard. And with Supreme Court rulings reiterating that we are a "Christian nation" (1892 Church of the Holy Trinity vs. the United States), we find confirming evidence of our national identity. We are one nation under one God, and this is still the Union standard. Consistent with our true foundation, we still hold these truths to be self-evident. And as we look forward to a coming family reunion, it too will have a Union standard. _Isaiah 11:10_ reads _"And in that day there shall be a root of Jesse, which shall stand for an ensign of the people; to it shall the Gentiles seek: and his rest shall be glorious."_ The two sticks will become one, and they will be under the reign of Christ. And when that happens, a symbol . . . an ensign . . . a flag . . . a standard will be raised to define the battle lines and rally both nations to the cause of Heaven. It will not be defined by revisionists or globalists. It was defined long ago by Almighty God. It is sealed in the courts of heaven, and God is merely waiting for us to fall in love with His idea. This coming union will have a standard, and together the House of Judah and the House of Israel will be one nation under One God. I present to you the Union Standard:

The two sticks have become one in God's hand. On the flag, 13 stripes represent the 13 tribes of Israel. They have rejoined and colonized in America, and they are Zion. The lone Star of David portrays the one God who presides over the affairs of our Union, and His name is Jesus Christ. You see, "In God We Trust" cannot be removed from America's DNA, and it cannot be removed from Judah's DNA. This is why the symbolism from both flags is embedded in this flag. It is not mere words; it is who we are. In the meantime, may we learn what it is to be one nation under one God.

CLOSING ARGUMENTS

In matters of right and wrong requiring a decisive verdict, the opposing arguments may end up as a case in a court of law. Throughout the trial, the one prosecuting the case is presented with a challenge. In the simplest of terms, their job is to collate all the evidence at their disposal and present it in an easy-to-understand format to the jury. Because it is a court of law and not a court of feelings, the emotions of the jurists must be rendered secondary to the facts as they search for the truth in their deliberations. How they feel about the case matters little. Whether-or-not they like the players involved matters little. Justice is only served when they base their verdict entirely on the evidence presented. Many juries have been duty-bound to handle matters of life and death, and for the rest of their lives they live with the emotions associated with the verdict they handed to the judge. But in the deliberation room itself, feelings are not to be regarded in their search for the truth. They must decide on which side of the law the case falls based on the evidence presented.

As you have read this book, you have been the jury and I have prosecuted my case. Now it is time for you to make some decisions. To be presented with truth, and dismiss it, is not recommended. Conversely, to be presented with error, and not challenge it, is also not recommended. Too much is at stake in either scenario. You must take a stand for the truth, and make it your personal conviction. Acquiescence to a teaching because Grandma believed it is not good enough. You must believe something for yourself because you have studied it and proven it to be truth. It may be hard for some to imagine, but sometimes Grandma was wrong. Ultimately, time will prove everything I've written in this study to be right or wrong regardless of what anyone thinks about it. These events will be fulfilled precisely as God has declared them, and the task of searching out what they may look like before they occur is a challenge placed in the hands of fallible men. Lest you think that a *"whatever will be, will be"* approach is the best route to take, consider the words of <u>*Proverbs 25:2*</u>; *"<u>It is the glory</u>*

of God to conceal a thing: but the honour of kings is to search out a matter". When fallible man searches out the mysteries and veiled truths of scripture, God considers that to be an honorable pursuit. Even if we struggle on the path to find the truth, the whole truth, and nothing but the truth. A right understanding remains possible with the right foundation, and this is why the final book of the Bible is named *The Revelation*. God does not intend for understanding to be hidden from mankind or He would have named His final letter The Hidden, or something else along those lines. Instead, He has devoted a considerable portion of His Bible to revelation. God desires to reveal to us how events will transpire in the end of days. A *"whatever will be, will be"* mindset is typically the result of laziness, an unwillingness to confront the tough issues, or an unwillingness to be wrong. Of course nobody wants the latter, but if we want to be on the front edge of the wave we must search out the truth and stake a claim based on what we discover. And we must do so before we get to the time of their fulfillment. That journey may even require challenging the status-quo thinking of the day. Consider the words of Solomon.

Proverbs 4:

> *5 - Get wisdom, get understanding: forget it not; neither decline from the words of my mouth.*

> *6 - Forsake her not, and she shall preserve thee: love her, and she shall keep thee.*

> *7 - Wisdom is the principal thing; therefore get wisdom: and with all thy getting get understanding.*

Our quest must be for truth, it must be relentless, and it must take place while the sky is still blue and time is still available to build an ark.

And speaking of arks, we must be willing to act on what we discover, because faith without works is dead. *Proverbs 22:3* says *"A prudent man foreseeth the evil, and hideth himself: but the simple pass on, and are punished"*. Prudent men and women still build boats. God gave Noah a revelation, but He did not provide him with a boat. Noah had to build that himself to weather the storm. He had God's revelation, God's instruction, God's design, and God's help. But it was Noah's ark. The thing that separated Noah from the rest of the crowd was not information about what was coming; it was his willingness to alter his lifestyle accordingly. The moment Noah told the people that a flood was coming, they too had the same information that he had received directly from God. Think about that for a moment. Here were heathen men and women, and they were afforded the same information that Noah had received. They were not looking for it, but they got it anyway, and therein lies the mercy of God. They were even given a period of time in which they could repent and change their ways. But they did not believe the information presented to them and they continued living unaltered lives. So the difference was not in the knowledge heard, but in how they believed and how they handled the knowledge.

Noah believed it and acted upon it, even at the expense of being called a fool because he was not a part of the establishment. According to the political and religious establishment of his day, he would not have been considered normal. But then again, neither was Jesus. The establishment usually (and incorrectly) assumes that because it is the biggest kid on the block, it is the right kid on the block. It has the most money, the most power, and the most people; so obviously it is correct. This is the driving force behind all things politically or religiously correct. The establishment determines what is normal, right? Frankly, nothing could be further from the truth. For Noah, the coming deluge was a greater reality than the blue sky above and any drumbeat the establishment was beating. He was marching to a different tune, and it shaped his actions accordingly. And he was the only one who was right. I'm sure his family was thankful when it rained, but I wonder if they were just as thankful when they were missing out on some great blue-sky parties. When the judgment came, the political and religious establishments of that day were swept away in the deluge, and only Noah and his family survived. Noah did not have many followers, he did not have a television ministry, and he did not have a lot of friends. But he built his world around the truth and that is what mattered most. It is a reminder to us that the establishment is not necessarily our friend, and cozying up to it will rob us of the resolve necessary to act appropriately to the revelation we receive. The fullness of time will come. And when it comes, the events of scripture will be fulfilled as God has decreed them. My hope is that you have been given a revelation of what is upon us and you are willing to alter your life accordingly. How God asks you to respond will be His revelation, His instructions, His design, and He will help. But it will be your boat.

If you consider dismissing my case, first ask yourself a couple of questions. What if I am right; and what if I am wrong? If I am right, you have a lot to think about and prepare for. If I am wrong, the events will still occur. There will be a Beast, a Temple, and an Outer Court. And you will be in one of them. You had best get to work defining what and where they are, and get into the Temple. There will also be an alliance of nations that attacks the House of Israel. You need to get to work defining who all the players are and position yourself accordingly. There will be a Woman who is spared, and a son of perdition who arises in the Temple. Start defining them because these things will occur in the locations where these entities exist! The primary thing in question comes down to this; are they coming soon to a street corner near you, or will they occur in other locations in distant lands? These are the questions you must consider if you want to dismiss my case.

If you hold to the prevailing traditions of men and determine that the House of Israel is the Jewish State overseas, what will you do with America? If you believe we are Mystery Babylon, you have no foundation from which to defend America or stand up for her. To be fully Christian is to love what God loves and hate what God hates, and according to the scripture Mystery Babylon is an entity that God despises. So you should too. If America is the great harlot, you should be rooting for her demise. You can do so hypocritically and find yourself in the company of Obama's Pastor, Jeremiah Wright, who urges God to damn America yet still covets her blessing. Or you can choose to cheer her downfall from afar with all strings detached. If America is Babylon, move. Move now. God's call is for his people to come out from among her, so get with it and get out. If you believe it, act on it and don't look back. But before you do, remember that you will also have the monumental task of explaining how America was birthed as one nation under God and how we have been blessed above all nations of the world. How is it that the number one missions-sending nation in history is dotted with churches from sea to shining sea; yet we are somehow an evil plot from hell that is despised by God? The two positions do not jive. Welcome to the jury ☺.

If you determine that we are not Mystery Babylon, but also not the House of Israel, you still have a dilemma. How did the greatest nation in history sneak on to the world scene yet the Bible says nothing about it? Are we a lucky anomaly? Are we a giant afterthought to God, and unworthy of any mention? Where did the 'saac's sons come from, and how did we get here? Why did we come here? Why would God say so much about lesser nations like Iran, yet say nothing about the central nation in human history? Like them or not the Saxon people have shaped the events of history like no other people, and their colonization must be somewhere in the Bible. These are the struggles you now face, and if you handle them with the facts, they are good struggles to undertake. Are we Babylon or not? Are we the House of Israel of not? We are the House of Israel and I have presented evidence to that end. Remember that as a jurist it does not matter what you feel about that. It may be an inconvenient truth for many, but truth is more important than its degree of convenience. Render your verdict based on the facts alone, and let the chips fall where they may.

If you, like I, have come to the conclusion that America is the House of Israel, it may be a hard truth to face. As seen in this study, the implications are enormous. Paul told Timothy in his day to "*endure hardness as a good soldier*". In our day, we too must be willing to handle the truth and any degree of hardship associated with it. America's toughest days are yet to come and you have come to the kingdom for such a time as this. The history books have not been closed, and another Washington, Adams, and Revere will rise to the occasion. America's next generation of minutemen is in the making right now, and perhaps you are one of them. Regardless of the role you will play, you will not endure by being soft, passive, and in the closet with your convictions. Like our forefathers, you may be required to draw a line in the sand and pledge your life, your fortune, and your sacred honor to America's defense. To the bold and to the fearful I only have this to say; feel the fear and do it anyway. Your only option is forward into the battle. So you may as well embrace the implications and prepare accordingly. And by the way, don't forget to wear a smile. We are entering the time of *Daniel 11:32* which declares "*the people that do know their God shall be strong, and do exploits*". That is something to smile about, and God may have had you in mind when he inspired Daniel to write that verse. It may be your name that is penned in the annals of history as the one who turned the tide in the coming fight. This will require a firm resolve like

David had when he faced Goliath. You may be the only one willing to face Goliath, and you may look utterly silly standing there all alone and vastly outgunned. But in that situation it really stinks to be Goliath . . . IF . . . you know your God and His Word. I pity the hordes who face the men and women who have been commissioned by God to make their stand. You will not be able to do so unless you have the conditioning of a soldier. Soldiers are not made in easy chairs; they are made by undergoing physical and emotional rigors that others never experience. They live lives of discomfort while the majority live in comfort. They go to war while civilians go to the mall. And this enables them to stand in defense of their nation when the battle comes. Enduring hardship in the good times is what makes them useful in the hard times. Now is the time to train your mind, your body and your soul for the battle ahead. Now is the time to be alert and ready, and it is with this intent that this book has been written. *1 Corinthians 14:8* says that "*if the trumpet give an uncertain sound, who shall prepare himself to the battle*"? This book has been a distinct sound, and I have endeavored to blow the trumpet in Zion. Alarm clocks are not necessarily liked, but they are needed. I am calling on you to stand in defense of this nation.

Lastly, I do need to address the emotional fallout that comes with this knowledge. Throughout this study you have seen that the prophets tell the same story. Ezekiel reveals the assaulted-then-protected entity to be the House of Israel. When we arrive in the New Testament, it must tell that same story somewhere, or one of them is not telling the truth. But as you have seen, it does tell the same story, and John reveals the House of Israel as the Woman and the Temple. If you understand that and it resonates within your heart, you are "seeing" it with the eyes of your spirit and you now enter the company of the prophets. The prophets could "see" what others did not see, and this is why they were called seers. But their spiritual sight also brought with it some emotions that others did not feel. Daniel "saw" into the future, and the gravity of what he saw made him sick and unable to perform his normal duties for a period of time. He was witness to events that would take place thousands of years into the future, yet he felt them with such intensity that he felt as if they were imminent. He even had to take some sick-leave just to process what he had seen. When Nehemiah "saw" that it was time for the restoration of Judah his mood changed. He wept, fasted and prayed over his nation. His countenance was troubled to the point that the king of Babylon noticed. Had the king not been favorable towards his cup bearer, it could have cost Nehemiah his life. And then there is the story of Elijah. He got so discouraged that he ran away from his duty to deal with a corrupt government. He ran from the queen to a cave, and there he asked God to let him die. He was worn out from standing in defense of his nation. These are all feelings associated with prophetic sight, and they are the signs of what I call prophet's disease. Prophets see and feel truth that the majority around them do not see and feel. And they see it and feel it with an intensity that affects their emotions. It just goes with the territory and there is no amount of happy talk that can eliminate it. Even the thought of confessing a new Cadillac into their garage holds no appeal. To men and women with prophetic sight, the message coming from the <u>First Church of I Love Me and I'm Wild About Myself</u> does not hold their interest. It is too narcissistic and too fluffy. How can they be pacified with a new Cadillac when their nation is on the verge of its most serious days? That is the burden carried by prophetic men and women, and this is why their message throughout scripture was called the burden of the LORD. It may seem odd to most, but seers live in a different (real) world, and they are usually considered to be a little odd. They fast. They mourn. They build boats. They weep. But they that sow in tears shall reap in joy. God keeps track of those who weep for our nation, and while weeping may endure for a night, joy will come in the morning. A new day will come.

Until then, as you see and feel the events as they really are, you may find yourself sitting in church on any given Sunday feeling like Noah would have felt at the yacht club. A schooner may be pretty, but it is insufficient for the coming storm. Because many churches have chosen to be non-prophet entities (no pun intended) they too focus on pretty little things that are insufficient for the days ahead. If the truth be told, the corporate church does not want people feeling any discomfort in the message they dish up. So they choose to splash around in the shallow end of the pool, serve up warm fuzzies on a silver platter, and remain unseeing. Yet the band plays on and men and women of understanding grieve for America. They can see a storm coming, and they can see that the priests are not weeping between the porch and the altar asking God to spare His people. Life goes on simply because they do not know . . . or worse . . . they do not care who America is in God's eyes and what the enemy is about to pull. They have chosen to be blind, and the big picture is not their frame of reference or the reality that is driving them. The sky is still a pretty blue, and there are bigger offerings to take for bigger buildings to build and bigger quotas to fill. Rest assured, the time will come when both the political and religious establishments will crumble, but from what I see in scripture it will not be until America is about to be overrun by the northern army. Only then will we be corporately desperate enough to do what God requires of us. Reread *Joel 2* if you have any doubts. Until then, may God give you eyes that see, ears that hear, and a heart to obey what the Spirit is saying to the church.

Court is now in session! To the Judge of the universe, we conclude with this . . .

"Your Honor, the jury has reached its verdict. And the verdict is . . ."